PARABLES

FROM

PATROL

Skinner —

I Hope you enjoy

PARABLES

FROM

PATROL

STEVEN SANDERS

TATE PUBLISHING
AND ENTERPRISES, LLC

Published by Tate Publishing & Enterprises, LLC
127 E. Trade Center Terrace | Mustang, Oklahoma 73064 USA
1.888.361.9473 | www.tatepublishing.com

Tate Publishing is committed to excellence in the publishing industry. The company reflects the philosophy established by the founders, based on Psalm 68:11,
"The Lord gave the word and great was the company of those who published it."

Book design copyright © 2014 by Tate Publishing, LLC. All rights reserved.
Cover design by Junriel Boquecosa
Interior design by Manolito Bastasa

Published in the United States of America

ISBN: 978-1-63122-823-0
1. Religion / Christian Life / Spiritual Growth
2. Religion / Christian Life / Personal Growth
14.04.01

CONTENTS

My ears had heard of you
But now my eyes have seen you
Therefore I despise myself
And repent in dust and ashes

—Job 42:5

INTRODUCTION

Working as a police officer, I see people at their worst. Sometimes, I end up seeing God at his best. I am an evil, evil man. I have no right to write about Jesus. I do this because I love him and am not ashamed to tell folks about how good he is. Jesus has been good to me when I have wronged him, denied him, and been ashamed of him. This book is not an attempt to make right the things I have done wrong. This is what I have to do because I can't keep it to myself.

Most of these parables are simple. A lot of them are goofy. God has chosen to reveal himself to me through simple and goofy things, and I hope whoever reads this book understands that God is trying to make himself known to us. If it takes speaking through the goofy experiences of a goofy guy, then that is what God will do.

On a completely unrelated note, the word *police* is properly pronounced like this po-leece with a strong emphasis on the *po*. If you use the more common puh-*lees* pronunciation, it ends up sounding more like *please* when you get all jacked up and yell it at someone. When I say it, I extend the *po* out extra long and add a "dang" before it just to add more emphasis and awesomeness.

THE DOG

I was driving around the ghetto one night when I heard what I thought was a woman screaming. I sped to the location and found that it was actually a small black dog being attacked by two big white dogs. I realize that I am not the animal police, but it got me all riled up. I hopped out of my car and yelled, "Hey fool!" at the big dogs. I guess that was the magic word because the big dogs walked across the street, sat down, and just watched me.

The little dog was in a bad way, but it was alive and able to move. I told it to run away. It just looked at me. I was like, "Dog. Really. Go." It was like, "Dude. Really. I don't speak English." I even tried making gestures. I'm sure it was quite a sight, but the dog would not budge.

I thought that if I drove away, the dog would take the hint and leave. But I knew if the dog didn't leave, it was going to get killed. I drove a few yards, and the dog didn't leave. I turned around and drove a bit further in the other direction. Still, the dog didn't do anything.

I couldn't hang out with the dog all night, so I left. After handling a call for service, I came back to where

I had left the dog. It was still in the same place, but it was lying in the street. Dead.

Long ago, Jesus rescued a woman from being stoned to death. Afterward, He told her, "Go now and leave your life of sin." What I believe that means is, we have been rescued for a reason. We are to run away from our old habits, or we will end up in the same spot again. Don't take the salvation lightly, and allow Jesus to transform you into a new creation and give you a new life.

He stands there, screaming at us to move ourselves into a different environment.

If only we would listen.

WHAT GIVES HIM THE RIGHT?

This knucklehead took a BB gun and shot up a bunch of businesses very early one morning. He just drove by and shot the windows out. No reason. He's just a turd. This caused thousands and thousands of dollars in damage.

My fellow police buddy, Nickell, found the guy driving around one night soon after. He initiated a traffic stop, but the knucklehead tried to get away. He failed and soon gave up.

Here is where it gets annoying.

During the mini-pursuit, a can of baby formula was spilled inside the knucklehead's car. He was madder than a wet hen. At himself? Of course not. At us? Naturally. He told us that we needed to pay for the spilled baby formula. Actually, it was that we "better" pay for it. Really. I can't make this stuff up. He caused thousands of dollars in damage by an intentional act of meanness. We were trying to stop him… you know, doing the whole police thing and one jar of baby formula accidentally spilled. We didn't make him evade, and we certainly didn't cause the spill. Still, he wanted his "rights," and he demanded that we replace the formula.

How dare that idiot get so offended about that stupid can of formula after he had caused so much intentional damage to other people?

How dare I refuse to forgive anyone for what they do to me, when my sins caused the creator of the entire universe to die?

JOHN

There was this old time police officer named John on my squad when I was brand-new. John had been at the PD for like twenty years. When I came in to work after being off a few days, I was informed that John had been fired. It was a big mess involving sexual assault, explosives, and possible child porn. I guess "big mess" is putting it lightly.

So John was arrested. He was found guilty and was sentenced to prison. Real uplifting story, huh?

Here is the point. When John stood before the judge, the judge did not ask him about his years of service to the city. He did not ask about the lives he had saved or any of the good things he had done. None of that mattered. He wasn't on trial for doing good things but for bad things. The question was, had John committed the offenses for which he had been arrested? The answer was yes, and he was punished.

When we die and stand before God, the question will not be about how much good we have done. The question will be if we have committed any single bad thing. We will be on trial for all the wrongs we have done throughout our lives. There is no scale of good versus bad. There is no accounting for good behavior. There is no measure of how bad we were compared to someone else. God will ask if we have done even one thing bad. Our good works won't account for a dang thing.

If our answer is that we have ever done wrong, and it will be for everyone, we only have one hope. Jesus died as punishment for everything that we have done. If, when we were still alive, we accepted his death as payment for our sins, the record of our wrongs has been erased. We will be like totally sinless, perfect little beings. It is only after our sins cannot be found that anything good we have done will be rewarded. If we did not trust in Jesus when we were alive, we're up a creek. No amount of good work will cover even one sin.

I am going to stand before God when I die. Yes, I have done an unholy amount of bad things, and God has seen every solitary one. When God asks me how I plea, the answer will be simple. I won't plea guilty. I won't plea not guilty. I will only plea the blood of Jesus.

TITA

I had this dog named Tita. She was a pug, and I loved her. It probably bordered on being weird, but she was legitimately my best friend.

When I was still in training, my field training officer asked me about my personal life. Was I married? Negative. Girlfriend? Negative. Gay? Negative. I told him that I had a dog. Predictably, he asked me what kind of dog I had. I loved my dog, but I realized that saying I had a pug made me seem less macho. You know, a pug really doesn't epitomize manliness. So I gave a weak answer.

"I have a pug, actually. But, you know, I've had her since I was a kid… my sister actually bought the dog, and it kind of adopted me." I was embarrassed to talk about my pug. Like announcing that I had a pug would mean I was weak or less police-like.

The truth is, that dog would have died for me. No matter how annoying I was, the dog was there for me, was keeping me company, was always happy to see me, and would have proudly claimed me to all her smashed-faced pug friends. I was ashamed of her.

Man, was I a schmuck.

I really felt like I had let her down. You know, like she heard what I said and understood that I was embarrassed to claim her as my own. As lame as this sounds, I had a hard time facing her later that day.

I got home, and Tita was happy to see me. I felt like a worm.

Being a Christian is nothing to be ashamed of but a lot of us are. It isn't cool. It isn't tough. It isn't (insert whatever word you hope describes yourself). But Jesus isn't ashamed of us. I have no idea why not, but he isn't. He is very clear, though, on how he feels about us being ashamed of him.

"If you deny me before man, I will deny you before my father" (Matthew 10:33).

FAKE KISS < JESUS

Some people just have it bad. Their lives are just crappy. Their family sucks. Their job sucks. Everything sucks.

I know a few people like this. One is a taxi driver named Jean.

I worked at a KISS tribute concert one night. Not being a fan of KISS, I wasn't a fan of the impersonators. Not being a fan of bars, I wasn't a fan of my life that night. Jean showed up. Man, was she pumped. I have seen her several times over the course of my career, and I had not ever seen her smile until then. She sang along with the band, headbanged a little, pumped her fist in the air, and shouted with joy and victory.

It was kind of cute.

While Jean was rocking out, a waitress of the bar came up to me. She started talking about how stupid Jean was because she believed that this was the actual KISS band. Apparently, Jean had come up to the waitress earlier all excited and awestruck because KISS was right in front of her. The waitress just made fun of her and then walked off.

It broke my heart. How terrible must her life have been when hanging out in a dingy bar and dancing to a KISS tribute band is the highlight?

Look around. If the best thing in your life is getting to watch a fake KISS band in a smoke-filled bar in West Texas, it may be time to do something different. Jesus offers us fullness and a great victorious life. It's not all roller coasters, bull riding, balloons, and beer, but it's good. If everything else in life sucks, Jesus is still good. He is much better than KISS impersonators.

THE TROUBLE WITH MIRRORS

There is a guy at the PD named Fred. Okay, so his name isn't Fred, but I can't use his real name. Fred is that guy who can't do anything right. If by chance he does something right, it's by accident. To top it off, he really thinks highly of himself. If Fred is reading this, he does not think it is about him.

Fred has great intentions, but everything he does turns to manure. He's classic Barney Fife. No one respects him. Not other cops, not bad guys, not anyone. If he were to save the whole world from imminent destruction, he would still not get any respect. I gave the guy the benefit of the doubt when I first met him, but he turned out to be a certifiable dufus.

You know, it's fun to crack on Fred. A lot of what he does is so bad that it's entertaining. Everyone makes fun of him. The nicest people even hate on him.

One of the reasons that I talk about Fred is because I want the focus to be on him and not on me. If everyone is looking at Fred and talking about how stupid he is, they will miss the thousand stupid things that I have done. It's a sound strategy that works dang near every time.

Another reason that I talk about Fred is because the people I like also talk about him. I want these people to like me, so I can't take up for Fred and be seen as an idiot-sympathizer. Friendship and association with him must be avoided at all cost.

Here is the problem. Well, there are several problems, but here is one of the most obvious to me: I own mirrors.

When I was a kid, I practiced pro-wrestling interviews in the mirror. In high school, I practiced pick-up lines in the mirror. In college, I practiced sermons in the mirror. These days, I practice interrogations in the mirror. I have always danced, kicked, and flexed in front of the mirror. Suffice it to say, I like my mirrors.

But looking in the mirror means that I have to look at myself.

And I have done many of the same things that Fred has done. I have seen other people do the same things that Fred has done. Are we universally mocked for doing the same things? Not usually and I am not sure why. I guess it's because all of us cool kids are busy pointing out the speck in Fred's eye and ignoring the plank in our own.

That dang plank sure does get in the way when I am telling my reflection how awesome I am.

TESTIMONY

I hate testifying in court. I always get real nervous before I get on the stand. It doesn't help that I naturally talk insanely fast, mumble, and stutter. When I add my nervousness to my already jacked up speech, the result can be disastrous. One time, they had to change out court reporters mid-trial because the one originally assigned to the trial couldn't keep up with me. No joke. I felt like a jerk, and there wasn't anything I could do about it. The judge even griped at me and told me that I needed to try harder, but I was hopeless.

A fellow officer and I got into a fight with a dude who had beaten up his wife and then threatened to kill her. The bad guy came at us swinging, and the rodeo was on. Eventually, he was subdued and arrested. That was the fun part.

Months later, I had to go to court and testify that this wanker had assaulted my buddy. That was the *no fun* part. I was very nervous. This bailiff came out of the courtroom and talked to me at one point while I was waiting for my turn to testify. I don't know if his job was to patrol the hall outside the court, or if the nervous shaking of my legs was vibrating the entire building; but either way, he struck up a conversation. He asked me if I was nervous. I told him that I was.

He said, "All you gotta do is tell the truth. I mean, you aren't gonna get up there and lie, so there is nothing to be nervous about. Just tell the truth."

I waltzed into the court and just told the truth.

The dude got fifteen years in prison.

I guess that "tell the truth" stuff worked.

So many of us, myself included, are nervous about telling people about Jesus. I think that I will screw it up, come across as preachy or pushy, lose a friend, get fired, be made fun of, or made to look like a fool. But all we have to do is tell the truth. It's really that simple.

With that in mind, here is the truth...

My life sucked until I gave it to Jesus. I didn't even really know what it all meant, but I told him that I needed to give him my life. Since then, my life has sucked a whole lot less. In fact, it really hasn't sucked at all. Even the hard times aren't that bad. It just isn't like it used to be. The difference is that I have been made into something new, so I see things differently than I used to. I really believe that I can do all things through Christ who strengthens me. That is my testimony.

MY FAVORITE STORY EVER

Hedrick, Doug, and I were riding with a narc in an unmarked car, trying to arrest this really bad dude. He was supposed to be armed, so we were all sporting assault rifles. It's simple math: bad guy plus gun equals more than one cop plus bigger guns. And when the fecal matter hits the rotating oscillator, it's just more fun to have your friends and an AR-15 to share in the glory. The plan was to pull up behind the bad guy's car when it stopped at a red light and then jump out and nab him.

Our camouflage must have not been so great because he jumped out of his car and ran away before we ever pulled up behind him. I didn't see the guy running away, but Doug, who is secretly a ninja, did, so we all started running down the busiest street in town, shouting and cursing. People talk a lot of trash about cops being slow, but we were all pretty fast runners. Unfortunately, we were wearing gun belts, combat boots, and polyester, and we were carrying rifles. He was wearing tennis shoes and had a head start. Guess who won that race.

We lost sight of the guy for a few minutes and began checking the area. Suddenly, T-Weezy called over the radio that he had our bad guy detained nearby. Irritated because we had been outrun, the three of us ran to that location, ready to crack his skull.

When I arrived, I saw the guy lying on the ground, rolling around, and moaning in pain. My first instinct was to kick him, but I saw T just standing there looking at him. I found this odd, so before I violated the poor guy's civil rights, I asked T what he had done to the guy already. He held up his hands and said, "I didn't touch him."

Upon closer inspection, I discovered that the guy was holding his crotch and was crying, "Oh my nuts! Oh my nuts!" There was a pointy metal fence just a few feet away, and the bad guy had jumped that fence whilst evading the police. He had cut his jeans. And his undies. And his... self.

From the police perspective, he needed to be arrested. Man to man, however, what was I going to do to a guy with one testicle dangling outside of his torn scrotum? He went to the ER that night instead of jail.

If I was more spiritual, I would be able to tie "dude nearly loses a nut while running from me" to a Bible verse. I'm not that good, but I am more than satisfied with the justice that only God can give.

A CITY ON A HILL
CANNOT BE HIDDEN

I've read the Bible completely through at least three times. Much like *The Complete Book of Wrestling*, I don't get tired of it. There are parts that I skim like genealogies, parts that I skip like the building of the tabernacle, and parts that I read over and over and over like Samson killing people with a donkey's jawbone. The point is, in all of my reading, I have not found a definitive list of "cuss words." My reading comprehension skills can lack at times, but I don't recall a scripture that says dropping the F-bomb is a sin. Still, it's essentially universally accepted that Christians aren't supposed to use certain words. I really don't know why, but I do know that the use of such words typically leads to people calling us hypocritical.

At various times in my life, I have been rather liberal in the use of profanity; but for the most part, I have tried to keep my language clean. I made it through the police academy and nearly the first year of patrol without using any profane words at all.

A few years into my career, I was assisting with the police academy's physical training. One particular guy really wore on my patience. He always had something to say, and it was never anything worthwhile. So I told him to "shut the——up and run." It took about two seconds to say. I haven't forgotten it years later.

Word quickly spread around the PD that I had cursed at some recruit. Everyone else in the history of mankind had done the same thing, but it was newsworthy because it was the good Christian boy who had done it. People who had not been there and had not really ever spoken to me asked me about it.

Way to go, Sanders. Way to spread the love of Jesus.

The Bible refers to the follower of Jesus as a city on a hill. It explains that a city on a hill cannot be hidden. It's not that Christians *shouldn't* go unnoticed, but if we are living for Jesus, we *can't* be unnoticed. People are going to see what we do, and it will reflect directly on their view of Christians as a whole and probably also on their view of God himself. The world is waiting for us to screw up, so they can point out how stupid our beliefs are. I am sure that everyone except for me has forgotten all about me cussing at that kid. Heck, I've said a whole lot more bad words since, to be honest, and I'm really not sure if everyone here at the PD knows that I am even a Christian. Dang. That sucks to say.

Christians, the spotlight is on us. Don't——it up.

THE PERFECT FAMILY

Policing in the same town where you grew up can make for some awkward moments. I went to a disturbance where this kid from my church had beaten up his mother. When I asked him what the deal was, he started crying and said, "Steve, in church we seem like the perfect family, but we aren't." No joke. First off, I didn't live under a rock, so I knew that his family had fallen apart years earlier. I had also kept this kid in the church nursery when he was little, so I had firsthand knowledge that he was a turd.

He went to jail, and I drove off with a new thought. Why do we pretend to be perfect at church? Can't we show up with the expectation that the people around us know that we are screwed up and still accept and love us? Sure, I wear a suit and tie to church, and a pro wrestling T-shirt and flip flops everywhere else, but I don't want to hide who I am when I walk into church. If I spent all Saturday night working a case where a twelve-year-old boy was sodomized, I don't want to see you on Sunday morning and say that I'm doing great. I want to tell you that life sucks, and I want to shoot someone.

Some Sundays, I really don't want to be in church. I'm tired, cranky, fighting with my wife, stressed out, and not feeling it when I am asked to clap my hands to "This is the Day that The Lord Has Made." I don't want to whine to you, but I also don't want to pretend. The best sermon I ever heard was when the pastor said to his congregation, "My sister is in jail. Please pray for her."

The church could be a support structure for people who need it. It could be a place where you feel safe enough to tell someone when you want to kill yourself. It could even be a place where people worship God in truth. There's a concept… if I am going to truly worship God, the God who made me, the God who knows everything that I think and do, then I need to do so without fear of what the guy next to me will think. Plus, it isn't my job to impress him anyway. It's my job to worship God. It's his job to worship God and not worry if I think he's a weirdo.

If anyone from my church is reading this, here is some scoop—I'm a sinner, and I'm moody. I've done a bunch of bad things, and if you knew all about me, you would probably not talk to me for very long. I'm sure you are in the same boat. I've arrested a few of you, so I know how bad you can behave. The beauty of the Christian experience is that Jesus comes to us when we are screwed up, and he always makes us better. That said, as bad as we are, you and I are both less evil than we were; and if we stick with Jesus, we will only get better.

The perfect family is the one who relies on God to make it better and doesn't pretend to not need him.

NEW CREATION

In college, I worked as a crossing guard. I know, I know, this book is about police work, and a crossing guard isn't a cop. My boss at that time always told me that we worked for the police department, and I don't think Jane with Career Path would lie to me, so I'm just gonna go with it. Anyway, the job was pretty sweet for a college kid. I worked four hours a day and got paid $100 a week. Most of the time, I sat under a tree, rocked out to Jill Phillips, Saviour Machine, and Waterdeep, and did a lot of reading.

During my first year as a crossing guard, I was in a personal funk. I was depressed, confused, and significantly unhappy with life in general. When the school year ended, I couldn't find a job anywhere in town, and that just made my funk worse. It was a bad year, and one of the worst summers ever. It ended on a very high note, as I had a conversation with God that changed my life. He told me that it was time to really give my life to him. The concept wasn't new to me, but it suddenly seemed that way. My whole outlook on life changed and so did my personality.

The following fall, I went back to the same crosswalk. I wore the same camouflage hat, olive green cargo pants, and T-shirts. I also had very long reddish blonde hair. In my mind's eye, I was memorable (and dead sexy). Plus, that was my assigned crosswalk, and I had seen those kids and parents twice a day, every dang school day for months. I even talked to most of them.

There is a point, I promise…

So there I was, minding my own business, when a parent came up to me and told me that I was so much better than the guy they had the year before. I cocked my eyebrow and told her that I was the same dude, but she didn't believe me. She was really convinced that I was a different person.

This lady might have been on crack, but I walked away with an understanding of what being a "new creation in Christ" really meant. I'd been a Christian for all of my life, but when I finally gave everything I had to Jesus, I became something new. It was apparently evident in my life: how I carried myself, talked to people, and acted. I didn't just act like I was different; I really was different.

That is how I know Jesus is real. He made me different.

I DON'T UNDERSTAND

Christians are often asked some variance of the question, "Why do bad things happen to good people?" I think it's a fair question. You know, if God is so loving, why does life suck so much? The flip side of that question is every bit as fair but not asked nearly as often. That question is, "Why do good things happen to bad people?"

Many of my wildest early adventures involved working with Nickell. Nickell and I worked the same shift, and we hit it off pretty quickly. We also worked adjacent sectors, so we worked side-by-side most every night.

Nickell stopped this car with two dirt bags in it. Being nosey, I pulled up behind him to help. Not long after, one of the bad guys ran, and Nickell began chasing him. I wanted to chase too, but there was still one dirt bag at the traffic stop, and I would have hated for him to drive away with a load of dope and a dead body or something in his car. So, trying to be helpful, I told dispatch that Nickell was chasing a guy eastbound on Pleasant. Good information except that he was actually running west. Big help there, buddy. Nickell still tells that part of the story like ten years later.

Being the cheetah that he is, Nickell caught the guy with a slight assist from a questionable passerby who saw an opportunity to assault someone and get away with it. When Nickell brought the guy back to the car, he soon discovered that there was a problem. The bad guy told him that he had swallowed a bag of cocaine. Instead of going to jail, he was carted off to the ER, so he wouldn't die. He had swallowed the dope as soon as their car was pulled over. If he had not run and subsequently gotten caught, he would likely have been released from the stop and then died minutes later. Attaboy, Nickell. You legitimately saved a life.

Soon after, the same bad guy broke into a woman's house and raped her.

Too bad he ran that night. If anyone needed to die, it was him.

Why did that guy have to live? Wouldn't it have been better for everyone if he had just died the night he was arrested? Truly, no one would have missed him, and he wouldn't have screwed up that innocent woman's life.

I don't have a good answer. I could type out an answer about God's will being better than ours and there being a reason for everything, and I really believe that, but that doesn't help ease the pain very well. This much I do know: even when I don't understand, I will choose to believe that God is love, and God is just. I've been through some bad things, but Jesus has never let me down. Trust isn't always a feeling. Sometimes it's a decision.

My job is to do the right thing and let God be God.

UNREMARKABLE

This dude who was a husband and a father decided to use enough meth to kill himself, most likely by accident. Accidental or intentional, the dude still died. A subsequent autopsy was completed, and according to the medical examiner, "The gray and white matter of the brain are unremarkable."

I'm sure that, in this case, the term *unremarkable* means that there wasn't anything medically noteworthy about it, so he has no remark to make. Be that as it may, unremarkable is a term that can also mean "lacking distinction, ordinary, plain, or meh."

How sad would it be for someone to think of us as unremarkable when they look at our dead bodies? You know, our lives were just kinda there and didn't really mean anything. We didn't matter to anybody and didn't make a difference in the world.

I'm not the most important guy in the world, but I hope that my life leaves some kind of impact on somebody. I really want to save the world, to tell you the truth, but I may have to settle for just making it a little better. It would be awesome if some dude cut open my dead head someday and could see the fingerprints of God on the gray and white matter of my brain.

I bet he would make a remark.

DISCIPLINE

My first DWI arrest that I made on my own was terrible. My sobriety tests were done incorrectly, and I had no idea what I was doing. I had not yet been certified to administer the fancy tests, so I just winged it. It wasn't rocket science, but it might as well have been. Fortunately, the drunk driver was blitzed and could hardly stand. Plus, he told me he was drunk, and he had already peed on himself. Even I could work that case.

So I arrested the kid and put him in my backseat while I searched his car and waited for a tow truck. Later, I reviewed my video. In addition to seeing just how terrible my tests had been administered, I was able to listen to what the bad guy had to say while I was out of the car because of my fancy spy-like in-car microphone. The only thing I remember him saying was, "Oh, Jesus, help me."

The Bible tells us over and over that the Lord disciplines those he loves. I believe that because I can't ever get away with anything. What's more, the times that I have prayed for God to bless me, he has responded by showing me the areas of my life that are screwed up.

Money doesn't fall from the sky, I don't get promoted, my wife doesn't wait on me hand and foot, CM Punk doesn't stop by my house for tea, and I don't arrest my little sister's dirtbag ex-boss. Instead, I get discipline and correction. God makes me face my shortcomings and then gives me the grace to change.

I think Jesus helped that drunk kid by letting me catch and arrest him. No one got killed or injured, and that guy had to answer for doing what was wrong.

Jesus, help us all by not allowing us to continue to screw our lives up.

IS THAT IT?

A fourteen-year-old pregnant girl got drunk and decided to kill herself. Her family called the police, and I was one of the first guys there. Fain, who will always be one of my heroes, and I found her sitting on a balcony ledge with a knife to her belly. I was not afraid for my life, but I also don't take stupid chances, so I stayed back and gave her instructions. I just wasn't in the mood to get stabbed.

I started talking to her and trying to reason with her. Eventually, I asked her what was so bad. She answered that she wanted to kill herself because her boyfriend broke up with her. Before I could stop myself, my response flew out of my mouth like unsympathetic vomit. I said, with a tone of surprise, confusion, and unimpressed-ness, "Is that it?"

Go figure; she didn't appreciate my comment. She started screaming and stabbing herself. Very soon after, she was taken into custody.

I think I was trying to let her know how temporary her problems were. Teenage boys break hearts every day. There are plenty of other fish in the sea, and some of them aren't turds, so this really wasn't the end of the world. The problem was that to her, it *was* the end of the world.

Sometimes people need to be reminded that their problems are really not worth stressing over. Other times, people just need someone to listen to them. Obviously, I am not much of a counselor. I am working on listening more and giving advice less. I don't know everything, but sometimes I forget that. I also forget that people don't expect me to know everything, and I rush to speak up to direct their lives. I have learned, mostly the hard way, to hold my tongue more often and listen when people are hurting.

The book of Proverbs reminds me that even a fool is thought to be wise if he just keeps his trap shut. Apparently, Mr. T was right all along when he yelled, "Shut up, fool!" back in the 80s. Who knew he was a prophet?

STEVE! WE'RE LEAVING

Patrol is the greatest thing ever except for SWAT. The only actual goal I had when I became the dang police was to get on the SWAT team. I'm not much of an athlete, and I am not consistently a very good shot; but after three years on patrol, I made it onto the team. Our team in Midland is a part-time team, which means that we all have other jobs at the PD, and we do SWAT whenever necessary. Our team, for right now at least, is divided into two entry groups and one sniper group. My team leader is Fincher. I do whatever he tells me to do, exactly how he tells me to do it because: (a) he's the boss, (b) he's a lot better at SWAT than I am, and (c) I'm scared of him.

We were SWAT-ing a house one fine day, and the guy hitting the door was having trouble getting it open. Fincher turned to me and yelled, "Steve! We're leaving!" In all my time of training and experience, we have never just left a house because we couldn't get a door open. Our job is to get inside, and we make it happen. But without even thinking about it, I turned around and started to walk away. Looking back at the situation, it didn't make any sense. But, at the time, my thoughts were: (a) Fincher said to leave, (b) I do whatever Fincher says, (c) I'm scared of Fincher, and (d) Fincher called me "Steve" instead of "Bones." Since when does he know my actual name? As I was walking away, I realized that I was the only one doing so. I started to think that either I misunderstood something or everyone else isn't nearly as scared of Fincher as I am.

Then it hit me.

The sentence was, "Steve! Relieve him!" as in, I was supposed to take the ram from the guy that was hitting the door and start hitting it myself. Before I could act on my epiphany, someone else who had a better understanding of the English language had taken over.

We got inside, did our thing, and had a good time.

That, my friends, was blind faith. Everything around me and everything I knew told me that we didn't just leave if we couldn't get through the door. But I did exactly as I was told… or at least exactly what I thought I was told. No hesitation. No questions. I just turned and walked away. I trusted Fincher enough to know that he was always right, and my job was to do just what he said.

Do you know how wild life would be if we could trust God like that?

MY FIRST PROSTITUTE

My squad did this undercover sting at a sleazy apartment. The word was that we would be able to score some hookers, which sounded like a heck of a way to spend a Wednesday afternoon.

We met up with this goofy dude named Willie. He was apparently the neighborhood pimp, and he told us that if we were patient, he could get us some girls who were "gud lookin' and cleeeeeeean." Those were his actual words and pronunciations.

It was a very long process, and I ended up not even being in the room when the girl, whose name was Birdie, was brought in. According to Geo, the officer who made the deal, she told him that she would "take it up the butt and then down the throat for a crack rock." After throwing up in his mouth, Geo made the arrest.

Part of the reason behind this chapter is shock value. Part of it is humor. Part of it is to show how screwed up people can get. I don't think this lady began her life like that, and I think that if she were to step away and evaluate her predicament, she would not be game for all that nasty stuff just to get a tiny bit of cocaine.

Unfortunately for Birdie, she was too hooked on the rock to realize how jacked up she was.

Never smoke crack. Nothing good ever comes from it. That isn't in the Bible, but probably only because crack didn't come along until thousands of years later. When curiosity, peer pressure, rebellion, or whatever comes along and tempts you to smoke crack, think of Birdie and what she would put in her mouth to get it.

Ew.

THE WRONG QUESTION

When I am introduced to new people, it is usually like this: "This is Steve. He's a cop." My wife is introduced like this: "This is Kristyn. Her husband is a cop." Her occupation pays much more than mine, and it requires much more schooling and work than mine does, but it isn't mentioned.

After the introduction, the next topic of discussion is pretty well set in stone. It starts when the person I am meeting says, "You know, I've always wondered something. How fast can I go over the speed limit before I get a ticket?" The answer is Zero, actually. Folks don't believe me, but that is the real answer.

Now, I get that people want to drive fast. Heck, that's one of the reasons that I love being the dang police—I drive really, really fast sometimes, and it's awesome. I also get that people want to know what they can get away with. It's like telling a white lie, cheating on your taxes, flirting with a married woman, taking candy from a store, or peeing in the front yard. Is anyone really getting hurt, and does it really make that big of a difference?

Well, yes it does.

I'm a killjoy, but the question of "how much can I break the law and get away with it" is the wrong one to ask. The law is the law, and it's that way for a reason. There is a line in the sand that is not meant to be crossed. People cross that line all the dadgum time, and that is why we have the police.

Here is my actual answer to the question of speeding, just FYI. I, of all people, really don't get my dander up over people speeding. Typically, I don't pull anyone over for less than 7 mph over the limit, and it takes something pretty heinous for me to write a ticket. Every officer is different, but I just like stopping cars to see if I can take someone to jail.

God is much less gray when it comes to his law. I think that we, by our actions and inactions, ask God how far we go over his set limit before it technically becomes a sin. It brings back the whole "How far is too far" discussion that I heard all through my *True Love Waits* experience. Like the question of speeding, asking how bad we can act before we actually commit a sin is the wrong question to ask. Our focus should instead be on how far we can get from sinning.

The right question is, "How much like Jesus can I be?"

A SMALL REGRET

I went to a disturbance, but before I could arrive, the bad guy had left. The caller said that the bad guy was actually a bad girl, and she was wandering around the area drunk and stupid. I found this girl, and I soon discovered that the caller was not lying. It was a quick arrest, and we were off to jail.

I don't have any patience for drunks, but I am usually cordial with everyone that I arrest, at least until they push enough of my buttons. For whatever reason, I wasn't really nice to this girl. She was whining and crying in a typical drunken form, and I just didn't want to hear it or pretend that I cared. I don't remember how the conversation went, but I do remember that I could have been a lot nicer than I was.

When she bonded out of jail, she went to another town, stole a car, got into a high-speed chase with the police, and then crashed into a house and killed someone.

My first thought was probably, *Dang. I knew she was no good.* My second thought was, *If I had been nicer to her, would she have done all of that?*

It wasn't my fault that she killed someone. It was her fault because she is a criminal, and she acted in a dangerous way. I also really don't think that anything I would have said or done during our brief time together would have made an impact on her. So I'm not beating myself up here. I'm just wondering.

Every person has the opportunity to pass along love or hate to other people. I'm usually nice to people I don't know, and I save the hate for those that I love, which is stupid, but I digress. We should seize the brief moments that we have with other people, even people who suck, to show kindness. Some people need sternness and a butt whooping, but giving them tackiness and hate is different. There is a way to be hard without being hateful.

I don't usually regret being nice to people, but I always regret being mean-spirited, even when people deserve it.

BOOBIES

I'm not the best judge of character. I used to think that everyone was good and decent. Now, I lean more toward everyone being the devil. Sometimes, I am way off on my initial assessment of a person, but I always admit when I have made a poor judge of character. Here is an example.

The PD hired this kid named Frank. I liked him. He was smart and seemed to work hard. He laughed at my jokes too. He and I didn't work on the same shift, but I knew enough about him to know that he was a good guy.

Or not.

Frank got fired because he went to a domestic disturbance call and tried to get the female party to sleep with him. Really. Dude just came out and said it. Go figure. She didn't appreciate it, and she complained. A short investigation revealed that he had actually sexually harassed a whole heap of women, and he was soon fired and facing criminal charges.

Lots of other guys have thrown away their careers over trying to get laid while on duty. Police officers are handed the world and given the authority to wreck shop on bad guys, and some of them would rather chase boobies. I'm a dude, and I like boobies just fine, but putting bad guys in jail is what I get paid to do. For the record, the only boobies that I really appreciate are attached to my wife. Read the previous sentence again, Kristyn Ruth. These guys are throwing away years of work and years of future work for a few seconds of booby fun. Just doesn't make any sense to me.

Jesus gives his kids the world, and we often throw it back at him. There is no end to the greatness of what God has in store for those who love him and have been called according to his purpose. It's better than boobies, and it's even better than putting people in jail. It's better than anything we could imagine.

THE HOW-TO-BE-THE-DANG-PO-LICE PSALM

Sometimes, I need a reminder of how I'm supposed to behave. When I do, I read Psalm 101. Because I'm a heck of a guy, I have included it in this book so that you don't have to run away and look it up for yourself. See? I'm a total public servant.

I will sing of your love and justice; to you, O Lord, I will sing praise.
I will be careful to lead a blameless life – when will you come to me?
I will walk in my house with blameless heart.
I will set before my eyes no vile thing.

The deeds of faithless men I hate; they will not cling to me.
Men of perverse heart shall be far from me; I will have nothing to do with evil.

Whoever slanders his neighbor in secret, him will I put to silence; whoever has haughty eyes and a proud heart, him will I not endure.

My eyes will be on the faithful in the land, that they may dwell with me; he whose walk is blameless will minister to me.

No one who practices deceit will dwell in my house; no one who speaks falsely will stand in my presence.

Every morning I will put to silence all the wicked in the land; I will cut off every evildoer from the city of the Lord.

PERSPECTIVE

I was driving around one night, thinking about how terrible this town was. It seemed like everyone was drunk, violent, mean, and frikkan annoying. I started talking to God and telling him all about it. As I talked, I turned down a residential street. I noticed that there were so many houses on that street, and none of the people inside of them were calling the police at that moment. At the time, there were like a hundred thousand people in Midland; and I was contacting, I don't know, maybe fifty or so people on an average night. I don't do math worth a hoot, but that's a pretty small percentage. God showed me that my perspective was jacked up, and that most people in Midland weren't my enemy. The issue was that the people I dealt with weren't exactly the cream of the crop of the society, and I had just gotten used to only seeing criminals everywhere I looked.

Last Sunday, our preacher delivered a sermon about Christians sometimes needing a new perspective. Essentially, after life has kicked you in the teeth for a long period of time, it's natural to get discouraged and disillusioned. The timing was pretty funny because there were a few criminals in the congregation that morning, and I had spent the entire first half of the service mad about never getting a break from bad guys. I spent the second half noticing all the other people, who far outnumbered the criminals, and I really liked a lot of them. It made me much less crazy.

I've always thought the phrase "count your blessings" was pretty cheesy. The concept behind it, however, is right on the money. Looking at and focusing on all the things that don't aggravate you off instead of the things that do is like a breath of fresh air.

PRAYING IN THE ER

I pulled up to a bar fight and found the instigator wandering around, bleeding from the nose. He was drunker than a skunk, so I arrested him. The jail made me take him to the ER for medical clearance, which was irritating, and we ended up waiting in the ER for a few hours.

While we were there, the man started to have a divine revelation. It may have been inspired by the alcohol or by the arrest, but he wanted to talk about God. At the time, I was single; and all I really knew anything about was God, police work, and pro wrestling, so I was game for the discussion. Our conversation went like this:

HIM: Sanders, you're a good man.

ME: Thanks.

HIM: You believe in God?

ME: Yes.

HIM: Jesus Christ?

ME: Yes.

HIM: The blood of the cross?

ME: Um, yeah... I think I get what you're saying.

HIM: Pray for me, Sanders.

ME: Okay, I will.
HIM: Right now!
ME: Okay.
HIM: Put your hands on me and pray!
ME: Wow. Okay.

So I put my hands on him and prayed in the middle of the ER. I asked God to direct his life, heal his nose, and help him to be better. While I prayed, he closed his eyes, mumbled along, nodded his head, and cried.

When it was over, he thanked me and said, "I feel the spirit of God in you."

In all my life, I don't think I'd ever been told that. Again, the guy was hammered and very emotional, so I didn't get all weepy or super spiritual or anything. I just nodded my head and waited for the doctor. Eventually, he was checked out and cleared for jail, so I loaded him up. I dropped him off with the jailers and told him to behave himself.

It may have just been the beer talking, or it may have been legitimate. Without forgetting all of the circumstances, I choose to believe what he said. Our conversation and prayer made me want to be a better man and live a life worthy of the spirit of God.

CAN GOOD WORKERS BE GOOD FATHERS?

I was the dang police before I got married. Working was all I really did, and when I wasn't working, I was thinking about working. I was often working on my days off, volunteering for overtime, teaching at the police academy, playing catch-up on a few reports, or something along those lines. Basically, if I was in town, I spent part of every day off doing something work-related. Plus, I always came in early and stayed late. It was this way for six years.

Then, I got married. My wife, for whatever reason, didn't think that me working on my days off was as fun as I did. Plus, having someone at home actually gave me a reason to be there and not at work. Still, it was hard to adjust to not working every single day and to coming home on time. It was as if not being totally available to the police department every day was a betrayal of my calling.

To be completely honest with you, my wife, and myself, I still have a hard time not putting my job first in my life. I know, I know. The good Christian boy is supposed to put God first, family second, and work somewhere much later. It's not just that I love my job, it's that I love to work, and being a good employee is very important to me. I'm always willing to "take one for the team" at work, but that means that my family, which as of right now also includes two very young sons and a bun in the oven, has to be put on the back burner some days. I was late to my oldest son's first birthday party because I was working on a robbery. He didn't care, but my wife was unimpressed.

My dad didn't seem to have this problem, which gives me hope. He worked all the time, and when he was home, he was working on a project, but he was still very accessible. If my dad was not around, I knew it was because he had to work, and I don't think I ever took it personally. One difference is that my dad wasn't madly in love with his job like I am with mine.

I can think of at least two guys here at the PD who are terrible workers but seem to be good husbands and fathers. One of those guys used to work a patrol sector next to mine. He always went home on time, even if it meant that I had to stay late to work something in his area. He took care of non-work-related stuff on duty even if it meant that his actual patrol work had to be done by me. It never seemed to phase him a bit that he screwed me all the time for the sake of himself and his family.

I see my work as a representation of my family's name. The harder I work, the more respect my family is given. I'm sure my perception is off, but I think my wife and kids would be ashamed of me if I didn't come to

work and give it my all, even if it meant missing something they had planned.

There has to be a balance of my family and my work
that I am missing. Kids, when you read this, know
that I love you more than my job, and one way I show
that love is by being the best worker I can be. I hope
you understand.

FRED'S REVENGE

Citizens can ride along with patrol officers sometimes. For them, it's exciting. For us, it's usually a drag. If the rider is someone we know, it can be a blast and can give them story-telling fodder for years. If it's some random dude, it's like having a stranger in your bathroom while you poop.

I made it a practice that when people showed up at the PD and asked to ride out, I usually volunteered. I didn't really want a rider, but it made me sad to think that they were all excited and were treated like a pest. I've always had a bleeding heart.

So this random old dude showed up and wanted to ride. He sat in the back of the briefing room, and the sergeant asked for one of us to take a rider. No one wanted the guy, and it broke my heart, so I took him. You know, I think those wankers I worked with knew that I was a big softy and would cave in eventually. I feel so used…

I pride myself of showing riders, even the annoying ones, a good time. Before long, we were speeding along, jacking up people, making arrests, and wrecking shop. I was also explaining to him why I was doing what I was doing just to make it more interactive for him. He was going to have some fun and learn something, dang it!

Remember my coworker Fred? This guy had ridden with Fred before. He loved Fred. Fred was the measuring stick by which all other cops were graded. He told me all about how great Fred was. He also talked about how lame I was. Talk about a kick in the gut. I thought it was the other way around—I'm the cool one, and Fred was the goober. Not according to my rider. Oh no, Fred was a top cop, and I was a poor replacement.

God has a way of keeping me in check. It's hard to be full of yourself when some random stranger tells you how much you suck at the thing you were born to do. I am not meant to think more highly of myself than I should, and looking back, I appreciate the lesson in humility.

It still hurts my feelings. I am a big softy after all.

CODY

My first foot chase was of a juvenile who had just assaulted his mother. I had gone to the same house about a week earlier, and the kid was gone when I got there. This time, I *may* have driven a *little* faster to get there when the call came out, and I arrived just as the turd was leaving. He saw me and took off. What I remember about the chase are the odd things I was thinking. It felt surreal. I was also worried about sounding like a girl on the radio. I had no idea which direction I was running, so I was very glad when I caught the kid and dragged him back to my car.

On the way to kiddy jail, the kid told me that I had no idea how it was living on that side of town. I was, he told me, from the suburbs. First off, little idiot, Midland doesn't have suburbs. Second, I spent the first twenty years of my life living about six blocks from where I had caught him.

I'm sure that what the kid was trying to say was that his life was difficult, and I could not understand his predicament. I know, from personal experience, that being fifteen years old is never easy no matter how much money or how many parents you have. A friend of mine, Cody, had things harder than I did at that age. His life had always been more difficult than mine, yet he has thrived. He put himself through college, got a job, got married, and has kids of his own. He continues to apply himself and reach for higher goals all the time.

Some people look for excuses to explain their bad behavior. Being poor doesn't cause us to hit our mothers, the devil doesn't typically make us do it, and it's still wrong even if we were "just born that way." We are responsible for our actions, no matter how screwed up we are by our situation.

Each one of us will be held accountable before God for the lives we lived. "I was poor," "I'm Joe's brother," and "You are from the suburbs" aren't going to impress God. If you think about why you do the things you do, and you see shortcomings in your actions, you can make a change. Just don't ruin a good apology with an excuse.

TRUE NORTH

I think that east should be north. I'm all jacked up.
When I look at a map, all I see are a bunch of lines
that don't mean anything, and I can never turn it the
right way. No matter what, when I step outside and
look east, I think that direction is north. I always have.
The fact that I know better doesn't change how I feel.

I was in a very short car chase. In any car chase, we
have to tell dispatch what is going on, and they typically repeat whatever we say so that everyone is clear
and knows where to go. The conversation went like this:

ME: We're southbound on Wall.
DISPATCH: 10-4, south on Wall.
NICKELL: Bones, Wall runs east and west.
ME: Okay, we're going… west?

Fortunately for me, Nickell, dispatch, and everyone
else working that night, the bad guy stopped immediately after, and I didn't have to make any more guesses
as to where I was going.

No matter how much I want to be right about east
actually being north, I am wrong every time. I can tilt

my head, close my eyes, do a dance, and scream, but east will never be north. The world just does not revolve around me and what I want.

The lesson about not being the center of the universe is a hard one to learn. The rules aren't going to change just because I don't like them. Once I finally realize that it isn't all about me, and life really is all about Jesus, I can start really doing some good in the world.

THE MISSION FIELD

My favorite calls to work on patrol are domestic disturbances. I don't like the drama, but I like putting people in jail for beating their spouses. Sometimes, however, the call isn't fun at all. I went to one where this woman had been beaten by her boyfriend. He was gone when I got there, which meant that I wouldn't be arresting anyone. She was very dramatic. I wasn't involved in the fight, but she seemed over the top with her emotions and her "woe is me"-ness.

There were two kids in the apartment too. One of them was in grade school, and the other was like four. The mother decided to pack up her kids and go stay somewhere else for the night. She was screaming at her kids to hurry up, she was screaming at her ride about life not being fair, and she was screaming at me without giving much detail as to what had happened. She wasn't doing anything productive—just screaming.

I watched as her older son packed up some clothes in a backpack. On the floor was a worksheet that I recognized and remembered from my school days as math homework. He picked it up, looked at his bag, looked at the worksheet, shrugged, and set it back on the floor.

In the grand scheme of his life, what did math homework matter to him? His mom had just been beaten up by her live-in boyfriend, most likely right in front of him, and doing math was probably pretty low on his scale of importance. Plus, his mom was screaming at him like the whole thing was his fault. I really don't think she could see past her own drama to see that her kid needed his mother.

I thought about how, if the kid even made it to school the next morning, the teacher would scold him for not having done his homework. He'd get in trouble, probably miss recess and thus his only chance to constructively burn off his frustration, and then act up in class because his life sucked so much. So the school might call his mother, which would add to her irritation, and she would beat the crap out of him when he got home.

Is it any wonder that kids grow up without a clue as to how to behave? I know I just preached about how circumstances aren't good excuses for acting badly, and this seems like a contradiction. We are still responsible for our own actions; some people just don't know any better. This is why we need to take Jesus to the street. We don't have to go around the world to find a ripe mission field. People need help right here.

LEVITICUS

Cupid, who was one of my favorite people to work with, and I responded to a call of an out of control eight-year-old girl. It is not uncommon for parents to call the police on their children, but eight years old is ridiculous. It sounded pretty dumb to me, but I'm a good soldier, and I go where I'm sent. When I got there, I learned that the bad seed had thrown a ceramic apple through a window and then scratched, "I hate you, Mom" into her mother's car. This was some serious *Omen* crap.

At the time, I did not have any kids of my own. I didn't really know how to talk to kids, but I had done this type of call before. I had tried a variety of methods. I've screamed, cussed, condescended, been their buddy, whatever came to mind. But this girl was different. I saw a Bible on the coffee table, and I had just read Leviticus 20:9 that morning. Things were about to get weird.

I asked the girl if she believed in the Bible. She nodded her head. I said, "Good!" and then I grabbed the Bible and started to read. "'If anyone curses his father or mother, he must be put to death. He has cursed his father or mother, and his blood will be on his own head!' See that, little girl, your parents can kill you, and it will be your own fault! They'll be all killing you, and you can call the police and say, 'Help, my parents are killing me,' and I'll say, 'Good!' and then hang up on you!"

Okay, so it was odd and probably not totally appropriate. She just sat there and nodded her head while her parents looked on in confusion, and Cupid just shook his head. With a few more "you're gonna die" comments, I finished my sermon and left, really hoping that no one would be killed. I could see the headlines:

Parents Kill Their Eight-Year-Old Daughter
After Advice from Cop and Leviticus

To my knowledge, they never called the police again. It could be that she straightened up, or it could be that they are still busy shaking their heads and wishing I had never come into their house.

My work here is done.

NOW THAT I HAVE SEEN

For as much as I love my job, I get tired of the drama and the drunks sometimes. I'm naturally very non-confrontational, and some days, I would like it if the world took the advice of Rodney King and just got along. On one particularly dramatic day, I thought that I had reached my limit. For a few seconds, I debated walking away from being the dang police and finding a job where I didn't have to always deal with annoying people and their overly dramatic, alcohol-fueled antics.

The problem with just walking away and pretending that everything is fine is that I have seen how bad the world is, and I am faced with a choice. I can either ignore it, or I can try to do something about it. I can't unsee what I have seen. I can't unknow what I know. I will always be responsible for doing something.

For every annoying criminal, there is someone innocent who lives in a peaceful little happy world and is oblivious to the carnage around him. It is my job—it is the reason I was born—to stand between the bad guys and the good guys and do something. I'm not the toughest guy in the world; I'm just the guy who is willing. I am also the guy who is responsible.

WHAT FOLLOWS US HOME?

I have wondered before about what follows me home from work. If you will allow me to get all mystical for a few minutes, I will explain what I mean. I believe in demons, and I am convinced that they operate all around us and screw with us as best as they can. There have been, oh, I don't know, seven million movies made about demons and how they affect us, and I think Hollywood usually misses the point.

If I go into the house of a child molester, it is reasonable to assume that there is some kind of demonic force at work there. Adults don't typically sexually abuse little kids, and there are lots of hypotheses as to why some of them do, and I don't think there is one definite answer to cover all circumstances. But let's say that in the case of Jerry, our random child molester for this story, demons stay close to him and make suggestions about how he should behave. Jerry, after years of listening to these demons and not having any other positive voices speaking to him, believes what he hears and takes action. So when I come into his house, these demons see a nice kid with a good family and a lot of potential for disaster. Jerry's life is already destroyed, so they swarm over to me to see how they can ruin my life.

Cops have insanely high alcoholism, drug abuse, suicide, and divorce rates. I've heard that one explanation is that we are constantly exposed to the ugliest parts of society, and it just wears us down over time. Makes sense, but what if there is more? What if the evil forces that are at work in the people we deal with just follow us home and pick us apart over time?

It's just food for thought.

All mysticism aside, people seem to act in the same manner as whatever surrounds them. It's one reason that parents don't want their kids "hanging out with the wrong crowd." Negativity is contagious, and often times, so is criminal and immoral behavior, whether we intend to pick it up or not.

I need to make sure that the person I am is the person I am supposed to be and not a person that I would arrest. Demons, society, peer pressure, and the general hardships of life should not dictate how I live.

WELL, THAT GUY WAS WRONG

I went to a disturbance at a particularly sleazy motel one evening. I parked a few rooms away from the scene because of our fancy safety tactics and because I always get lost looking for motel rooms. As I walked up to the room, I heard a man shouting, "I can beat the (slang term for feces) out of you, and the cops can't do a thing!" I looked into the room and saw him standing over a female who was just sitting on a chair and sobbing.

This is the part of the story where I wish I was Arnold Schwarzenegger and had an endless supply of one-line jokes. Unfortunately, I don't. The punch line is that I just stepped into the room, pulled the guy out, and put him in handcuffs.

I don't know what that wanker was thinking, but he was wrong. Dang wrong. He either lost his dang mind, forgot which town he was in, or was just trying to dissuade the girl from calling the police on him. Either way, he went to jail once I got everything sorted out.

Life often tells us that there is no hope for us. Sometimes, life sucks and we feel beaten down and helpless. We can't always see the light at the end of the tunnel, and sometimes the light ends up being an oncoming train.

I promise you that Jesus can help. It may not be the help you thought you needed, and it may seem to never be on time, but it's still there if you want it. Once Jesus swoops in and saves the day, everything will make sense.

Steve Tudor and Laura Fields had this to say a few years ago, and they won't lie to you:

> Sometimes when the hour seems darkest, sometimes when everything goes wrong, sometimes when the whole world seems to come all undone, that's when his love is so strong. When all of the things you held on to suddenly aren't there anymore, when everything is changing, but I'm still the same, I feel like I can't go on anymore.

> Just when you thought it was over, and just when you thought it might end. That's when the losing, it turns back on you, and that's when the heartache begins. But the victory is just beyond the sorrow, and the winning is worth every tear. Jesus has promised, and he will prevail, 'cause he can touch you and quench every fear.

> Jesus, he never changes. Jesus is always the same. Your friends may forsake you and the world turn you around.
> But Jesus will never let you down.

THE END OF MY CAREER

In the police academy, we were told that almost anything we screwed up could be forgiven, but lying
would cost us our jobs. Up to that point, I wasn't
afraid to throw a lie around if it was convenient. I didn't
lie all the time, but if the need arose, I was not above
making something up on the fly. You know, no matter
how I write this, it just doesn't make me look good at
all, does it? That is a lesson in itself.

Another cop and I went to a disturbance about a
year into my career. While I was arresting the bad guy
in the front yard, a neighbor's dog ran over and bit me
in the leg. It was a small dog, and I just shook it off. It
didn't hurt much, and I really wanted to make the arrest.
I met up with that same officer later at the jail. He told
me that I needed to tell my boss about what had happened because he was going to tell everyone about the
dog eating my leg. Because I chose to be uninformed,
I did not know that I was supposed to report crap like
that when it happened.

So I met up with my boss and ran it down to him. I
told him that I didn't think anything of it, and I really
didn't care. He told me that, if I really didn't give a rip,

I should just go to the owner's house and check the dog's shot records to make sure everything was cool. And that's exactly what I did. He told me that the dog's shot were current, but he didn't know where the records were. Already embarrassed, I told him not to worry about it. I got back in my car and called the boss. He asked me if I had seen the shot records, and I told him that I had.

I thought I was in the clear, but I told my mom about the ordeal a few days later. She, being a mother, freaked out and made me go to the ER to get checked for rabies. On the way to the ER, I called my boss again and told him the truth. He sounded annoyed and he should have been. I had to meet with Animal Control, and everything became a much bigger mess. On the plus side, I didn't get rabies.

I knew my career was over, and it was all because I was an idiot. Not reporting the dog bite wasn't a big deal, only because I was too stupid to know I was supposed to. Lying to the boss would mark the end of my very brief police career. I had to write a memo to the chief of police about what had happened, partially because of the dog bite, and partially because I had lied. So in the memo, I used the phrase, "I lied and told the sergeant that I had seen the shot records." My boss's boss read that and told me that I should change it because that would follow me my entire career. I politely told him that I had already lied once, and I was not going to lie again.

Somehow, I wasn't fired for lying. My boss told me to be sure, and he stressed *sure* to tell the truth about everything in the future. I didn't tell another lie—not to him, my family, my friends, or even a bad guy—for years. I still flinch when I lie to criminals, even if it's for a good cause.

Dang. This story sucks. The shame still haunts me nine years later.

OPINIONS

When I was still in training, my FTO (Field Training Officer) and I made a stop on an obvious drunk driver. I walked up to the car and recognized the driver. He looked at me and said in a drunken slur, "Officer Sanders, I'm a detective where you work." Yeah. Great.

I had talked a lot of trash before then about not cutting any slack to other officers who broke the law. It was time to put up or shut up. Well, I shut up and ran back to my FTO, who was sitting in our patrol car, punching the roof. He called his boss, and his boss called his boss. It was decided that I would make the call on what to do—arrest him or give him a ride home. No pressure or anything, right? It was bull crap, but it was good for me, and I learned a lot from it. Being the new guy and not knowing that this wanker did this all the time, I made the call to give him a ride home.

In a public setting, other officers told me that I did the wrong thing and should have arrested him. In private, however, I was told that I did the right thing by protecting our own. Years later, that nonsense still annoys me.

The main thing I learned from that was that everyone has an opinion, and many people will judge what I do. If I go with what half the crowd says, I will make the other half mad. If I do what is publicly acceptable, I may be privately kicked in the teeth. What is a skinny bald kid to do? The answer is actually very simple.

Since then, when I have been presented with two unfavorable choices, I have done what I thought was right and taken whatever heat came my way. One way or another, I'm going to lose, so I might as well keep my dignity. There are people at the PD who I trust, and I will ask their advice if I need some help making a decision, but the rest of the people don't get a vote.

I will have to stand before God one day and give account for what I have done. God won't be impressed with my excuses about not wanting to make people mad at me. He expects me to stand firm and do what is right.

God's opinion is the only one that matters.

ADVENTURES AT ST. PAUL

I was sitting next to my little sister in church one morning. It must be known too that I only ever went to actual church services on Sunday mornings. I had worked the night before, and I was a bit worn out. I guess I left Earth for a minute because I was suddenly very confused about what day it was. Also, my internal monologue must have been turned off because I blurted out, "What day is it?" My sweet little sister turned to me, and with only a tad bit of, "Are you seriously this stupid" in her voice, said, "It's Sunday."

I seemed to fall asleep dang near every Sunday. If you are thinking that I was wasting my time by even going to church, you may be right. However, Psalms talks about bringing a "sacrifice of praise," and that was what I thought I was doing. It was a sacrifice to be in church after working all night, and although I nodded off, I tried my best to be attentive.

When I worked Saturday night, I always came to church in uniform. I knew that if I went home to change, I would make an excuse to get into bed and fall asleep. The gun belt also helped a little bit to keep me awake. Plus, I've always looked dead sexy in blue polyester.

So one morning I fell asleep in the pew. I only know that I fell asleep because my dad woke me up. Apparently, my head had fallen back, my mouth was gaping open, and I was snoring like crazy. I'm sure that did wonders for the preacher's self-confidence.

I always felt safe in that church—St. Paul UMC. It gave me a sense that there were still decent people in Midland, and that we were not all headed straight for hell. The people there loved me, supported me, and comforted me. I will never forget that.

NO DAYS OFF

My wife and I were leaving Barnes and Noble, minding our own business, when we heard some guys arguing. I looked around and saw this old man shouting at this slightly younger couple in the parking lot. You might think that adults, especially seasoned adults, could resolve their problems without the police getting involved. Many of them can, but I guess that day just wasn't the day for resolution. It looked like the two men were about to start fighting, so I waltzed over, lifted up my T-shirt to reveal my gun and badge, and intervened.

The issue was that the older man had backed his car into the couple's car, and he was refusing to admit that he was wrong. I ended up having to call an on-duty unit but only because I didn't have the Private Property Crash Form in my personal car. My presence as a police officer, even one in flip-flops, calmed the argument and brought about the peaceful resolution of the conflict.

We expect police officers to always be switched on. An off-duty cop in public is just a police officer who is working for free. That is a pretty generalized statement, and not everybody feels the same way, but I think the public expects us to not really ever be unavailable for action. Even on vacation, we might have to regulate. Don't believe me? Just watch Die Hard.

Some folks have the opinion that being a Christian is only a Sunday morning type thing. They can live however they want to the other 167 hours every week as long as they give one hour to sitting in church being a *good Christian*. In truth, we don't have the luxury of taking a day off from Christianity. When the Holy Spirit of God lives inside of you, you take him everywhere you go.

Christianity isn't just a set of beliefs; it's a lifestyle choice that is directed by love between God and us. No matter where we are or what we are doing, we are still in a relationship with God; and we need to act like it, even when it's inconvenient.

THE JERRY SPRINGER SHOW LIVES INSIDE OF ME

Speaking of geezers behaving badly, I went to a disturbance where this really old, rich, white guy had gotten into a physical fight with his daughter's redneck boyfriend in the front yard. After he told me the story, the old guy looked me in the face and said, "You would expect something better from me, wouldn't you?" I responded with, "Um. No."

Money, age, employment, or anything else won't make us immune to screwing up. We are all a really bad episode of *Jerry Springer* just waiting to happen. Ecclesiastes 7:20 tells us, "There is not a righteous man on earth who does what is right and never sins." That pretty much covers everyone.

Not that many of you will care, but I don't usually judge people when they break the law. Some people are just wankers, and I have no problem saying so, but most folks I have arrested were good people who made bad decisions. Whatever we do can be worked out with time and with the blood of Jesus.

I really didn't want to write that last sentence. I wanted to add something about how some people are going to burn in hell forever, and they deserve it. Hence the "usually" in the sentence about me judging people.

Just like with the guy in this story, there is still much work to do in Steven Sanders, and I may be just one crisis away from *Jerry*.

JUST THE BEGINNING

Once you get sworn in as a police officer, you suddenly have all kinds of power and authority. You can arrest bad guys, drive fast, shoot people, tell people how to live their lives, get half-priced meals at Whataburger, and carry a gun wherever you want to except for federal court. But the swearing-in ceremony is just the beginning. Some people seem to have been born knowing how to be good cops, but most of us have to learn. I have to learn everything, and I always have to learn the hard way. Just because we have this authority doesn't mean that we have any idea what to do with it. The cop that I was nine years ago is a far cry from the cop I am now, and that is due to maturing and experience.

Getting saved is the first step in being a Christian. Some Christians have a dramatic transformation and go from evil to wonderful in a flash. The rest of us have to learn how to live right. That comes from prayer, reading the Bible, and letting God work in our lives. If you want to be a better Christian, it is probably going to take a lot of time and work.

As a side note, new cops are often very annoying. It's the same with new Christians. Cops and Christians suddenly have this new life, and it's so exciting that it just makes them a little weird. They are also typically very enthusiastic, and we, old-timers, would benefit from being around their excitement to go out and save the world. It would be a shame to say that we used to be awesome, but now we just go through the motions.

I've been a cop for more than ten years, and it's been an awesome ride that has really just begun. For the Christian, the ride is eternal; and it gets better, and we get better, all the time.

SIGNS

After seven years on patrol, I became a detective. My plan was to go to detectives for a little while and then return to patrol as a much better patrol cop or patrol supervisor. As interesting as detectives can be, I'm just made for patrol.

So I was detecting one day, and I was working a deal where this gym employee had snuck in after hours, broken into the office, and stole some cash. In an attempt to find him, a uniformed patrol officer and I went to his last known address. The suspect was a very large black man, and a very small white lady answered the door.

I explained why we were there, and I asked if she knew the guy. She got mad at me and started acting all suspicious, so I asked if I could check for the guy in her house. I was dressed in plain clothes, but my badge and gun were in plain sight. She asked me how she could know if I was really a cop. Fair question, I guess, so I pointed to my badge, my gun, the guy in the fancy police uniform behind me, and the cop car parked in the street. It wasn't good enough for her. She wanted to see my business card. I pulled out a card, and she let us in the house.

A business card. Something that could be printed off of any home printer. Not the fancy badge, the scary gun, the awesome polyester get-up, or the dang police car. A business card was the evidence that she wanted, and the only sign that she would accept. I wonder what would have happened if I had not had any business cards that day. She might have believed I was a cop if I ran over her with the cop car.

I don't see anything wrong with wanting a sign from God. It can be hard to know what direction to take your life, and a tangible clue can sure be helpful. When we ask for a sign, though, we need to have our eyes open. Andy Gullahorn has a song called "Burning Bushes." The final line of the chorus is "Walking through the valley of a thousand burning bushes, looking up to Heaven for a sign."

Sometimes, we need God to hit us with a car to get our attention. Other times, we just have to look at the obvious.

COME ON, DUDE

"**I** go to church just down the street," I just heard a suspect say. It was right after he told me about how he has been having an affair with his friend's wife for five years. She had just accused him of rape, and he used their affair to explain why I would find his DNA inside of her. He said he was embarrassed to admit it to me, and he was terrified that his wife would find out, but he could just walk into the lady's house any time he wanted to and get serviced. The lady was a wee bit crazy, and her husband was a bit mentally disabled too. My suspect was a real class act. Nothing says, "Pillar of the Church" like banging the crazy wife of a guy who lacks the deviousness to figure out that you are the worst friend ever. In talking to the suspect, there didn't seem to be an issue with continuing the affair until she went all *Fatal Attraction* on him a few months ago.

So the problem wasn't that he was doing his wife, child, friend, and friend's wife wrong, it was that his affair was starting to be of inconvenience him.

> POINT 1: Nothing that is hidden won't eventually come out.

POINT 2: Bringing up church when you are caught with your pants down is lame.

LOOK IN THE BOOK

Most of us police officers aren't able to tell you where all offenses are in the Texas Penal Code. I know that assaults are in chapter 22, and intoxication offenses are in chapter 49, but that's only because I have written "Assault PC 22.01" and "DWI PC 49.04" about ten thousand times on booking sheets. I have the general idea of most criminal offenses, but I'm not able to spout them out word for word. I don't have to do all of that because I understand the concepts, and I know where to look in the book if I need specifics. I have my penal code nearby in case I panic in the middle of an investigation.

My approach to the Bible is the same way. Committing verses to memory is a great idea and a good way to spend leisure time. I used to have a whole heap of Bible verses memorized, and I really wish I had more verses in my head these days. Still, I understand Biblical concepts, and I have a good idea of where to go to find specifics. It would be cooler if I could just rattle off chapter and verse, but I'm not that cool anymore. I suppose this means that I should carry a Bible with me wherever I go, just in case I panic in the middle of a conversation.

Gun, badge, phone, pager, and Bible. Maybe I should start rocking a fanny pack again, just to hold all of my essential gear.

My poor wife.

NOT LICENSED TO DO SO

There is a theory that police officers shouldn't give people life advice because we don't have a license to counsel people.

That sentence is the dumbest thing I've ever read. No, wait a minute. I read a love letter that this dude sent to my older sister when she was in high school where he told her that he was burning incense to her picture as his "blue-haired goddess," and *that* was the dumbest thing I have ever read. This other thing is a runner-up.

Do you know where I would be if not for the informal psychological and spiritual counseling of several non-licensed people?

We all have a responsibility to help each other. Sometimes, that really sucks. I do people a disservice if I see them ruining their lives, and I don't tell them anything. I'm not a big fan of drama, so I usually turn a blind eye to self-destructive but non-criminal behavior that I see outside of work. I don't want to be that annoying guy who is always trying to be everyone else's parent, but I would really hate to be that guy whose friends went to hell because I didn't do anything to stop them.

FOLLOWING THE LEADER

I grew up in Midland, but I pretty much minded my own business. I didn't know where all the trouble spots were, I had no idea where to buy crack, and I didn't know that half of the city even existed. I went to school, work, and home.

On my second day of field training, I got to drive for the last half of the shift. We were parked in a parking lot while my trainer talked to his cop buddy, and I typed some reports. We got a call of a drunk guy trying to fight people in the street. Dispatch gave the address, but I had no idea where it was. Plus, you've read by now that I can't read a map to save my life, so I was hopeless. The cop talking to my trainer knew where it was, so I just followed him. We drove crazy fast, made a bunch of turns, and I was totally lost. I didn't look at the street signs; I just looked at his taillights until he eventually stopped and got out of the car. From there, it was easy to find the annoying drunk guy in the street.

It ended up being my first arrest for public intoxication. It was also my first entertaining transport to jail, but I will have to save that story for a less polite book. The whole ordeal was a blast and is actually my blueprint for working all subsequent PI cases. If I had not followed the other officer to the scene, I would probably still be driving in circles trying to find it.

God told Abraham that he would be the father of many nations, but he didn't tell Abraham all the ends of outs of how it would unfold. At one point, Abraham decided to make it happen his way, and thousands of years later, the world is a big mess. Seeing as how much better of a man Abraham was than I am, it's no wonder that God hasn't told me the end result of my life. There is no telling what ridiculous steps I would take to make everything happen on my own. I need to just follow where the leader leads me and not worry about where I will end up or how I will get there. He knows the way that I should go.

IF I DO NOT LOVE,
I AM NOTHING

I got into this business to help people. The idea of driving fast, carrying a gun, and chasing bad guys was an added bonus, but I really wanted to save the world. Cheesy? Sure, but it's as true as it gets. I loved people.

After years of dealing with boneheads, my outlook has changed, and I don't care nearly as much about people as I used to. I'm not really interested in hearing a sob story, and I'd just rather put everyone in jail.

If I was a better spin-doctor, I would point the blame on mean people, uncooperative victims, liars, stress, or something cool like that. Since I have never been very good at giving a believable excuse, I will just go with what is most likely the truth and blame myself. I have lost sight of why I get up in the morning.

Even with my attitude, I'd still do anything for people, probably because that's how I'm programmed. I get it from my parents and grandparents, so it's in my DNA. I don't even usually gripe about helping someone. I like to do it. The problem is that I do things more and more often without love as the motivation.

No matter what I do, if I don't do it with love, I'm not bringing any glory to God. If I'm not bringing any glory to God, then I'm not doing a dang thing to save the world. The point here is that I believe I am doing good work, but it would be even better work if I was driven by love for God and people, not just a love for justice and doing right.

SAVING A LIFE

Doug and I responded to a child molestation at a trailer park. The bad guy was the victim's neighbor, and he was supposed to be armed with a gun. Naturally, we got our assault rifles and went to work. The guy was sitting in his doorway, but one of his hands was concealed inside the trailer. Another officer distracted the guy, and Doug and I launched. Before the perv knew what was happening, he had two very angry, heavily armed men shouting at him. He was slow to comply, so Doug grabbed the guy's arm. Doug is at least 700 times stronger than the mere mortal, so he threw the guy into the air and then dropped him onto the ground. He landed with his hands beneath him, and he wouldn't give them to us, so we had the pleasure of making him give us his hands.

As a quick side note, I enjoy all the fights with bad guys. I don't look for fights, instigate them, or pursue them once the guy is under control. When a fight is justified, especially against a child molester, it's awesome. When you fight without justification, you're a thug. End of side note.

We brought the guy to the PD to speak with a detective. I don't remember if he confessed or not, but the detective went to work on the necessary jail paperwork. We left the bad guy in a small interview room and went down the hall to her office to sort out the details. There weren't any weapons in the room with the guy, per se, but I was about to learn the hard way that the room wasn't as safe as I thought.

Every couple of minutes, I came back to the interview room to check on the guy. On one trip, I found that he had hung himself.

Not good.

I ran into the room and untied the guy while I screamed for the detective. He wasn't breathing, so I began giving him a version of CPR. By that, I mean that I slapped him until he woke up and took a breath. He didn't leave my sight until I dropped him off at the jail later that night.

Of all the people in the world to keep alive, a child molester isn't the first candidate who comes to mind. The truth is, I didn't keep him alive just to keep my job. I kept him alive because I really didn't want him to die. Oddly enough, if he had pulled a gun on Doug and me earlier that evening, we would have smoked him in an instant and not felt bad about it at all. The roles we play can be very different minute by minute.

People come into our lives and need help. We can't pick who God sends our way or what God expects us to do with them. We can pick how we respond. Do we help or let them die?

JESUS IS COMING... LOOK BUSY

H ere in Midland, once we finish our field training, we are given our own patrol car to take home and use it for personal stuff in the city. There are some restrictions, of course. If you are going to drink and drive, don't do it in your cop car.

On my first day off after getting my car, I picked up my old pal Cody, and we started just driving around. I wasn't usually much for cruising the mean streets of Midland, but this was a special occasion. As we rode along, Cody giggled like a schoolgirl at the awesomeness of what we were doing. I giggled too, but my voice is much deeper than his, so it wasn't very schoolgirl-ish. Yeah, dude, I just said that. It's Okay, Cody, you thought it was funny.

We were cruising around, and we ended up behind this giant black pickup. A little kid suddenly stuck the whole top half of his body out the rear passenger side window and started waving at us like crazy. He was all smiles, and it was hysterical. It got even better when the driver saw what was happening and noticed the cop car behind him. He immediately reached into the backseat and jerked that kid back inside and then hustled to get him situated in a child seat.

We laughed until we cried. I didn't stop the guy and give him a ticket for having an unrestrained child. I could have, but I couldn't stop laughing. Either way, the problem was fixed.

People act differently when there is a cop car behind them. I do it too. In fact, one time very early in my career, I was driving my cop car, at work mind you, and I suddenly hit my brakes when I saw another cop car behind me. It's just automatic.

We tend to act differently when we think Jesus is watching us too. The funny part about that is that he is always watching us. He has seen every dang thing we have done. Every. Dang. Thing.

He loves us anyway. No matter how many times we have watched porn, snorted cocaine, cheated on our wives, lied on our taxes, stolen from work, driven home drunk, planned a homicide, or lived in any kind of way that denied our beliefs—Jesus has seen it all. And he has been right next to us. And he still loves us. How can we not love him back?

We shouldn't act differently because we are being watched. We should act differently because we love the one who watches us.

CAN I GET AN EXAMPLE?

I was an obvious rookie. I had very little confidence too. I worked hard, kept a good attitude, and behaved myself, but I couldn't quite get a handle on the persona that I thought I needed to have to be a constructive and tough police officer. Bad guys wouldn't believe that I was as hard as they were especially because I had a stutter, looked like I hadn't eaten in years, and believed whatever lie they fed me. Being afraid to act wasn't the problem, it was being afraid of not knowing what to do, not being able to speak English, or screwing up the whole investigation. The main ingredient in "command presence" is confidence, and I just didn't have very much. Seeing my difficulties, an FTO told me that since I had no idea how to be a cop, I should find another cop who I respected and then act like him. I figured that I had nothing to lose, so I gave it a shot.

I'm a firm believer in being my own man and marching to my own beat, but I needed some direction. I started taking certain traits from other guys. One guy had a scary walk. I stole it. Another guy had a very calm but commanding stance. I stole that too. I wanted to take the authoritative speech of another guy, but I was hopeless in that field. Fortunately, Meat Loaf is right, and two out of three ain't bad.

It started working, and before long, I felt better about myself. I know, I know, it's goofy. How can the way a person walks and stands make him feel like more of a bad mamma jamma? I don't know, but it just did. Once I started believing in myself, bad guys started believing in me too. By the time I really had to jump into chaos and take control, it seemed like I was born to do it.

Starting out in the Christian life is much the same way. It's easier because you have the Holy Spirit to guide you, but it helps to be able to see someone who has traits you want for yourself. They are like Jesus wrapped up in the body of someone you can touch.

Surround yourself with people who are good for you. They will help you become who you were born to be.

WAKING UP DEAD

I watch too many action movies. The central charac-ters always have a lengthy death scene, there are lots of foreshadowing before we even get to that point, and it's pretty dramatic. Since I am always the action hero in my mind, I don't see myself going out in my sleep. I, of course, really don't have any say in how I am going to die, but that doesn't change how I see it all coming to an end. I don't think I'm alone in that way of thinking either. I'm sure that lots of people believe that they have plenty of time left on Earth, and they will get things right with God before they die.

The first dead bodies I handled as the police had been involved in a car crash. A guy was cruising along in his eighteen-wheeler when he probably fell asleep and ended up driving off an overpass. His wife had been in the sleeper portion of the cab, probably asleep too. Jimmy and I were still in training, so we got to do the grunt work. That meant digging through the wreckage and pulling out the bodies. The problem was that the driver had been hauling some kind of flam-mable chemical, so everything had burned to a crisp. He was a great big guy, and he was faced down in a pile of vehicle parts. It took Jimmy, me, and a guy from the funeral home to lift him out of the pile, and my job was to lift in the middle, right next to his exposed butt. I had been taught not to open my mouth around a dead body because the smell would get in my mouth and stay there for days. I tried, but I unintentionally grimaced during the lifting and caught a good whiff. Flame-broiled butthole became the worst smell I could think of for a few years after that. It has since been topped, but more on that later. His wife was much smaller and easier to get out of the wreckage, but I had to jump back in and find her severed leg.

Immediately afterward, we all went to eat. Go figure. Chicken fajitas will never taste the same again.

If that lady had been asleep in the vehicle at the time of the crash, there was no way that she knew what was about to happen. There was no scary music to warn her, no image of the grim reaper standing behind her, no nothing. She just went to sleep and woke up dead.

We have no idea when our time to die will be. We've gotta be ready right now because we don't have a guarantee that the next second will be ours to enjoy. I may not go out as a hero in a blaze of glory. I may die old, alone and crazy, surrounded by people who don't know or love me and won't tell of my exploits once I'm gone. None of that is really up to me. I can choose, however, where I will wake up after I die. I don't know what heaven will be like, but it's where I'm gonna be.

I hope all of you guys will join me in that very good place.

ACCEPTED TO BE MADE BETTER

Back when I first tried out for SWAT, I made it but just barely. I was made an "alternate" and was evaluated over time to see if I would improve by the time there was a permanent opening. That evaluation was actually done for all new guys, not just the ones who needed a ton of improvement. I'm a bit of a slow learner at times, so it took a while for me to catch up.

Because I was an alternate, I got a bunch of leftover gear. My vest was more like a dress. The pistol I shot was the oldest Sig Sauer 9mm piece of junk instead of the fancy SWAT-issued Glock. I used my patrol duty belt, which didn't function well with my SWAT tunic, and I wasn't issued an assault rifle. We'd be on the firing line, and I would have to borrow someone else's rifle to shoot when it was my turn. I was less like a team member and more like a groupie. I knew it was a necessary phase, and I am all about paying my dues, so I didn't feel slighted. I just wanted to be on the dang team.

After a couple of months, the other three alternates were made actual full members, and I was the only alternate left on the list. There were openings, but I just wasn't ready. Of the people at the PD whose opinions mattered to me, the SWAT bosses topped the list. If they didn't think I was ready then I wasn't. Still, it was hard to not get a little discouraged. Herman, the boss of the SWAT bosses, wrote each member's name on a board and divided them into teams for the foreseeable future, and I was the only guy in the room not listed on the board. Knowing my limited skill set, I understood. From an "I really want to make it on this team" view-point, it sucked. I took it like a champ, but dagnabbit it hurt, and I started thinking that I would never make it.

Then Herman handed me the most ghetto, Vietnam-era assault rifle, and he told me that it was being issued to me to use on operations. I almost did a back flip and kissed him. My rifle didn't have the fancy gadgets that the real members had, but my rifle might as well have been made of pure gold as I was that proud to carry my rifle home. I hadn't quite arrived on the team yet, but I was being included. They had not forgotten about me or given up on me. It was the single most encouraging moment of my career, and I knew that I was going to make it onto the team and accomplish anything else at the PD that I fought for.

Being made an alternate and then having to be trained up to make it as a full-fledged member meant that I was accepted as I was, and the team thought enough of me to invest their time and resources into making me better. As long as I listened to them and let them shape me into what they wanted, I was good to go. Almost eight years later, I'm an assistant team leader. It took time and work, but it happened.

That's how it is with Jesus. He loves you and accepts you exactly as you are, and he loves you too much to let you stay the same. He will invest his time into developing you into the absolute best that you can be. All you have to do is let him work. If the work hurts, the result is much easier to appreciate.

CRUTCH

I've written and rewritten this chapter a dozen times. I just can't make it say what I want it to say. I had the notion to ask God for help. The purpose of this book is for God to reveal himself to people using police stories, so you'd think that God would be a good resource for help.

Then I realized that I couldn't even remember the last time I prayed.

Dang.

A lot of people use the police as a crutch. They live their lives however they want, and then they call when they get in over their head. Gang bangers, crack dealers, tough guys, intellectuals, or even regular folks want to fix their own problems their way and then dial 911 for the police to come clean up their mess.

Fortunately for them, I'm happy to do it.

Fortunately for me, God is happy to come to my rescue.

Still, the idea that I use God like a criminal uses the police makes me want to poke out my own eyes.

FILTH

This preacher didn't show up for church on Sunday morning, and he had been sick for a while. That evening, no one had yet to hear from him, so some of the church members went to his house. They could smell something rotting inside the house from where they were standing in the street so they called us.

When I showed up, a senior officer was standing out in the street, just staring at the house. I could smell the house as soon as I got out of the car. Sheesh, it was bad. A sergeant, Big Ern, was in the front yard, and he was not looking very happy about the task before him. I was, and still am, too stupid and excited to care, so I charged ahead. I asked the other officer if he was going in, and he just politely shook his head. I knew I was going to find a decaying body, and I was probably going to puke, but so what? This was going to be pretty cool.

Big Ern and I went inside. He put a cloth over his nose and mouth and started down a hall. I checked the living room and kitchen. The floor was covered in plastic Wal-Mart sacks with food inside of them. Old, rotting, gross, stinking food. Before I could finish looking around that part of the house, I heard a crashing sound in the hall. Ern came running back toward the front door, bouncing off the walls and groaning, "Oh God," as he looked like he was gonna barf. Oh, this was going to be good.

I started down the hall and checked the first bedrooms. No sign of anything except for more rotting food. The hall came to a T with the bathroom on the left and master bedroom on the right. I figured he must be in the bathroom, so I went left. No body but lots of poop. It was smeared on the walls, toilet, and shower. I guess all of his toilet paper was in a plastic bag somewhere on the floor. I almost lost it, but I cowboyed up and continued.

I opened the door to the master bedroom and saw the body lying in the bed, totally under the covers. Made sense that he was covering up his face from the smell and ended up suffocating. Poor guy. I walked toward the bed, so I could survey the damage. Before I got there, the guy sat up! I almost shot him when he did that. I also almost did something else to myself that is one vowel different from "shot." He looked at me and asked me what I was doing in his house. I asked him what *he* was doing in his house. He didn't have a good answer. Heck, there wasn't a good answer.

The preacher was sent off for a mental evaluation, and I never heard what became of him. Before he left, he told me that he noticed the house was getting a little stinky, but he didn't think it was that bad. I bet that house stinks for years.

When you surround yourself with spiritual filth, it becomes harder to notice just how nasty everything is.

Eventually, everyone else will see (and maybe smell) your life and think that you are spiritually dead, but it won't seem like that big of a deal to you. If you don't get affected by the sins you commit, it's time for a spiritual evaluation.

COUNTING DOWN THE DAYS

I stopped and talked to this coworker of mine who is counting down the days until his retirement. He has it narrowed down dang near to the minute. It's crazy. His career has had its ups and downs, but dagnab, he's really looking forward to getting out of here.

There are times when I can't blame him. I get tired of all the bull, and I think about what I can do after I retire. But when I think about retiring from police work, the only thing that I really look forward to is not having to shave ever again. Most of the time, though, I just want to work. I don't think much about the upcoming years and what I will eventually become because I have too much other stuff going on right now that needs my attention.

I just heard a song by Bobby Chance called "Hold Back The Rapture." Bobby is always straight forward in his songs, so I can safely say that the point of it is that Jesus is coming back, but Bobby would like him to wait until more people can get saved. Whether you believe in a pre-trib, post-trib, mid-trib rapture, don't believe in the rapture at all, or you have no idea what the rapture is, it's safe to say that the world as we know it will end one day. A common theme among Christians is to look forward to Jesus taking us out of this world. I can't argue that being in heaven will be pretty cool, but I think we can get ahead of ourselves and miss the point of being on Earth.

What if we didn't focus on the restful future ahead and instead just put our heads down and went to work for the cause of Christ? How can I make the world less sucky today and how many people can I take with me when Jesus shows up to take us all home?

WOULD YOU LIKE SOMETHING DONE?

I became an FTO, and it was a blast. I was training this new kid, and he was struggling a bit. He was driving, and I'm pretty sure that I was running my mouth about some strange theory of police work. A car made a wide right turn and almost drove head-on into us. The kid swerved to avoid being hit and then kept on driving and shaking his head in disgust.

He said, "Man, I hate when people do that."

I said, "Was that illegal?"

He said, "Yeah. It was a wide right turn."

I asked, "Would you like to go stop him?"

He slapped his head, realizing that he was the police and he could actually do something about almost being killed by an oncoming car.

Everyone has the power to do something to make things happen. If there is something that you want done, often the best way to get it done is to do it yourself. If you think your church needs some kind of program to help other people, start one. If people around you need help, give it. God often puts people in our lives so that we can serve him by serving them. We should take action and not just talk about how someone needs to do something.

Be the someone who does something.

LOVE HANDLES

Don't let the man boobs and love handles fool you—I really like to work out. I don't exercise as often as I should, and it's usually because I wimp out and think of an excuse. I don't know why I do that. I enjoy exercise, and the PD makes us take physical assessments twice a year, so it's something that my job requires of me. I guess I'm just inherently lazy.

My soul needs some type of exercise too. This is a bit cheesy, I know, but that doesn't make it any less true. When I read my Bible and pray, my soul is strengthened. I might be using the incorrect term—soul, spirit, mind, intangible insides—I'm talking about that part of us that connects us to God. If we don't exercise that part of ourselves, we are killing ourselves worse than any greasy diet or lack of exercise kills our bodies.

We were made to connect with God in a healthy and vibrant way. It's actually very easy, but it takes time. I find excuses to avoid reading the Bible, which is pretty dang lame. I even enjoy reading the Bible, but I've been stuck in the book of Ezekiel for like a month. My soul just keeps getting fatter while I think of other things to do besides connecting with God.

If I want to be physically strong, I have to work at it. If I want to be spiritually strong, I have to work at it and be constantly connected to God. That whole, "I am the vine, you are the branches, apart from me you can do nothing" thing is legit. Any service that I do for God that is done without fellowship with him is like expecting an Under Armour shirt to make me thinner. It will fool some people, but if I stretch too much, my love handles will roll out and expose me for the fatty that I am.

Looks like I'm gonna go workout, shower, and then get back to Ezekiel.

WHAT IS ENOUGH?

Although I like dang near everyone I work with, there are only a few people that I actually consider to be my friends. These are the guys that I actually talk with beyond work stuff, and I value their opinions. A few of them have even proofread this book, and I am very grateful for their open and honest input.

I was talking with one such guy years ago, and we were discussing money. He told me that I should be rolling in cash because I was single and didn't have any kids. He wanted to know where all my money went. I told him about my spending habits (i.e. action figures and T-shirts) and that I tithed. He asked why I gave money to a church, and I told him that I was supposed to. I realize that God may not actually require us to support a particular church with our money, but the idea of a tithe is to give a tenth of our income back to God. Giving to the church where you are a member is the easiest way.

That concept shocked him. He wasn't against giving money, but he said that since we were technically risking our lives for people every night, our service to the community should be enough to satisfy a tithe. I disagreed, and I began to think about what level of giving of my time, money, and self to God is enough. Ten percent? Twenty? Fifty?

I guess a better question is, at what level of giving can I look at the bloody face of Jesus and tell him that I have given all that I need to give?

NO, DUDE, YOU WOULD NOT

This criminal told me that he would be a good cop because he was a good criminal. He believed that he would be able to catch all of the bad guys because he could think like them. He would be awesome at my job.

Um, no.

This isn't *Hardcastle and McCormick*. Criminals don't make good cops. Being a cop isn't just about catching bad guys. It's about not being a bad guy. It's about standing up to bad guys and keeping the good people safe. It's about being different.

Being a Christian isn't about following a set of rules, going to a certain church, or telling the rest of the world that we are better than them. It's about being set apart from the evil things of the world. We are going to screw up, but the core of who we are is motivated by a love for and from God.

It isn't about doing; it's about being.

BUSINESS IS BUSINESS

My wife's friend texted her one night to tell me that her husband was out driving around drunk, and that I needed to arrest him. I looked for him when I had some down time, mostly for his own good, but I didn't find him that night. I saw him the next morning. He had sobered up, and he said, "Hey, I'm sorry I put you in a weird spot last night."

I wasn't ever in a weird spot. If I had found the guy, I would have checked to see if he was drunk. If he was, I would have arrested him. If he wasn't, I'd have gone about my business. It was really that black and white to me.

Now, I liked the guy, but business is business.

Right before the battle of Jericho, an angel appeared to Joshua. Joshua asked the angel if he was for the Israelites or the other guys. The angel said, "Neither but as commander of the army of the Lord, I have now come." The army of the Lord was there to work, not to be friends.

I don't think God plays favorites. He offers everyone the same deal. People who take the deal go to heaven. People who don't, go to hell. If I was more educated, I would have some comment about predestination, but I'm pretty ignorant, so I'll leave that topic alone. When the question arises about how could a loving God send his own creation to hell, it's simple. Business is business.

MISPLACED FOCUS

This cop who was working as security at a bar arrested an obnoxious drunk kid for being, well, an obnoxious drunk kid. I showed up to transport the kid to jail, and we had to fight him to get him into the car. He yelled at us that we should be on the east side of town arresting (insert slang term for black people) instead of messing with him, as he was white and not really a criminal. The best part of this ordeal, aside from getting to pummel him into submission, was that his own mother was watching him act that way, and she actually walked up and slapped him after he said that. You go, lady. Get you some.

His point was that he shouldn't be arrested because there are so many other people doing worse things than what he was doing. That line is old and worn out. I'm really tired of it.

Comparing our sins to the sins of others is pretty common. In doing so, I can rationalize my behavior and tell God that I am way better than the guy sitting next to me. That way, I don't feel like such a worm.

The problem with that concept is that God doesn't compare us to others. He compares us to Jesus, and we all pretty much suck compared to Jesus. Our only hope of not ending up in hell is for Jesus to stand in for us in front of God so that God sees him and not us.

GETTING THIN

Once upon a time, I had a great head of hair. My hair was golden red, and it shined like the setting sun. I loved it, but I had to get a job. I tried a modified George Clooney for a while, but my hair would never lie down. You know, Dennis the Menace would not make a very menacing cop. So I started shaving it all off.

I started noticing that my hair seemed pretty thin in between shavings. I kept telling myself that it was just due to the shortness. To test my theory, I let my 'fro grow for a few weeks.

I was standing in line at a convenience store one night picking up my free "we love the police" cup of coffee. I looked up and saw a TV monitor with the store's surveillance footage running in real time. I saw the top and back of my head.

Stupid camera.

So yeah, I'm a bald son of a gun. My great plan to have Gandalf-ish hair when I retired wasn't going to happen. As soon as I realized that, the first thought I had was actually that there wasn't any point in ever retiring. I mean, heck, most days I'm happy to be the police for the rest of eternity, so it was a win-win situation anyway. If I had hair, I could retire and look like a bearded woman. If I didn't have hair, I'd become Methuselah in a polyester uniform. I'm good either way.

We all have an image of ourselves. For some of us, that image is not quite in tune with reality. When I ask God to reveal himself to me, I need to also ask him to reveal *my*self to me. I want to be real and see myself for what I am. How will I know what I am unless I have a brutally honest evaluation? God sees us from all angles, and he won't lie to us.

God, show us where we are thin and help us to be thicker.

GOOD EXCEPT

My wife is very open about the things I do that irritate her. My feet are gross, I don't pay attention, I snore, I'm forgetful, and my jokes can get really old. But I promise you that if you ask her directly, she will tell you that I am a good man. That's one reason why I married her. She also won't put a qualifier in her sentence after saying that I am a good man. She really thinks I'm good even if I do have creepy old man feet.

One thing that I have heard innumerable times from abused women is, "He's a good man except when he drinks." If that's the case, and if the case is that he still drinks, then he isn't a good man. It's harsh, and I probably sound like a judgmental know-it-all. Me being a jerk doesn't change the facts. If your man is good to you except he hits you when he gets drunk, then he isn't good to you. If he is good *except* anything, then he isn't good. If we see any exception to being good as acceptable then our view of what is acceptable is screwed up.

We can't be "good except." Not "good except" husbands, not "good except" fathers, not "good except" Christians. "Good except" equals bad. We have to choose how we are going to live. There is a line in the sand, and the one who drew it is even tougher than Colonel William B. Travis.

There is a difference in screwing up versus continuing a behavior that is wrong and making it an acceptable exception. Allowing an exception into our lives allows us to make excuses for being evil, and that crap is wrong.

JUDGES

My favorite book to sit and read in the Bible is *Judges*. It's just awesome. It's got blood, guts, sex, redemption, war, and a hint of gangsta rap. People make bonehead decisions in an attempt to fix other bonehead decisions, an angry long-haired man kills a bunch of wankers, a left-handed assassin loses a knife in the fat belly of a ruler, another ruler ends up pinned to the ground by a tent stake in his head, and the whole world just falls apart. Every so often, God fixes everything just to have people forget what God did and then everything goes to pot again. The whole book can be summed up in the final verse, which is, "In those days Israel had no king; everyone did as he saw fit."

I think God established laws and law enforcement to keep the planet from self-destructing. I enforce the laws of the State of Texas in an effort to keep everyone safe and keep society moving along. People, including the fat bald guy typing this sentence, are prone to do bad things to other people. Unfortunately, the moral code of most people isn't strong enough to keep us in line. We usually need someone to stand ready to knock us on the head if we do wrong.

Law enforcement is done for the benefit of the people. *Judges* is an awesome book, but it would be a real crappy way to live.

GRAD SCHOOL

A few years ago, I tried going back to college. All I thought about was work, dang near all of my buddies were cops, and I was becoming more of a hermit. I decided that graduate school would be good for me, as it would give me something else to think about and would broaden my horizons. My undergrad degree was Criminal Justice, and I thought that a master's degree in anything involving the police would be counter-productive to my goal. My minor was English, so I decided to pursue instead.

At first, it was a good change of scenery. It didn't take long, however, for me to realize that grad school was not for me. My teachers and classmates really liked operas. They used fancy words with seventeen syllables in casual conversations. They thought that reading a book by Mary Shelley was fun. One of the biggest red flags was when the guy who sat next to me announced to the class one evening that *Honkytonk Badonkadonk* was the dumbest song he had ever heard. I was definitely in the wrong crowd because that song is awesome.

Most nights, I had to work right after class, so I went to school in uniform. A classmate asked me, "Do you have to wear your gun to class?" I was, and still am, speechless. Do I *have* to wear a gun? Lady, I *get* to wear a gun.

I understand that the word *holy* means "other." I'm not saying that I was holier than any of my classmates because I carried a gun, just for the record. I was very much "other" from them, though. My calling and my life were so very different from theirs that it was ridiculous. Their lives are just as important as mine, so I'm not saying that I am better. Just different. Waaaaaaay different.

That's how Christians are supposed to be. Our lives should be so different from the world that we can't fit in even when we really want to. Our thinking should be different, our speech should be different, our everything should be different. People should be able to see our lives and tell that we are "other."

The whole *aliens and strangers* thing that the Bible talks about… it isn't a joke.

REPUTATIONS

In November 2005, I had to put Tita down. Yeah, she was a dog; but she was my dog, and I was very sad. My workweek started the next night. If I was more mature or better able to separate my emotions from my work, I probably wouldn't have arrested as many people as I did that first night back. My give a crap was broken, so if anyone gave me even a hint of a reason, I put them in jail.

It wasn't my finest day. I was probably rude to a lot of people.

If you have been around the Christian circle for long, you have probably heard about Doubting Thomas. After Jesus came back to life, he appeared to a bunch of his disciples. Thomas missed the first show, and when his buddies told him about it, he didn't buy it. He wanted to see Jesus himself and then put his hands into the nail holes before he would believe. Hence, Thomas is labeled as a doubter by people who have never met him. About a week before then, there was a discussion among the disciples about Jesus, who had not yet been killed, going to Jerusalem and if they should go with him. Thomas spoke up and said, in the Steven Sanders

Translation, "Heck yeah, we're going. If Jesus dies, we are going to die with him." He doesn't sound like much of a doubter there. He sounds pretty dang hardcore.

It's real common at the PD, and lots of other places, to label someone by a single interaction with them. Anyone who only met me the night after Tita died would not think much of me. I'm guilty of doing crap like that, and I'm not real open-minded about people once I have formed my initial opinion.

People say that Christians are sucky people. Some of us are. Some of us just have really bad days. Let's give each other a chance and some time to prove that the reputation we earned in that hour may not define who we truly are.

A BRIEF NOTE TO MY DAD

There was one night when everyone I talked to was crazy, drunk, a knucklehead, or a combination of the three. I had a few minutes, so I called my parents, mostly to vent about how terrible the world was and be dramatic for a few minutes. My dad and I talked very briefly, as neither of us really like to talk on the phone. He assured me that he was sane, sober, and not a criminal. I hung up and got back to work.

In a perfect world, I'd not be so dang emotional. If I was a better liar, I'd keep my feelings to myself. But we've gone this far together, so what the heck.

I had felt very much alone that night. I had decided once again that the entire world sucked. I was starting to not see a point to the work I was doing. But just talking for a few minutes with someone who was normal got me back on track and refocused on keeping bad people away from good people.

Thanks, Dad, for not being a knucklehead. You have been very good to me all of my life. You help me even when you don't realize it.

SITTING AND WAITING

Doug and I were riding around in an unmarked police car when we heard a call of a theft in progress at a store very close to where we were driving. The bad guy was described as "a black male in a gray T-shirt," and he was last seen running our direction. We parked and waited for him to run to us. Since our car wasn't marked, we could surprise and ninja him as soon as he got close enough. It was going to be awesome. Opportunities like that are better and come around less often than Christmas.

This old guy came jogging by. I thought that it was odd for an old man to be jogging in the heat of the day, especially through a parking lot. It was even more odd (Grammar Check keeps telling me that I should write "odder" but I can't bring myself to do it) that he was jogging in jeans. But, you know, people are weird, so I just ignored him. As he staggered in front of our car, Doug yelled, "That's him!" I rolled my eyes. Sure, he was a black guy in a gray T-shirt, but he was also 100, and he was not our guy. I've been doing this job long enough to know who the bad guys are and who is just in the wrong place at the wrong time. I turned to

Doug to tell him to settle down, but he was already out of the car and chasing the guy. I sat in horror as Doug got closer, yelling at this poor old man. The whole thing took like three seconds, but it seemed like three hours. The guy wouldn't listen to Doug's instructions, and he put his hand in his pocket; so Doug, not wanting to get shot, pointed a gun at him. I said out loud, "Holy crap. Doug's gonna kill this old wanker," and then I watched as Doug beat him into submission. It occurred to me that: (a) I was being a terrible back-up officer, (b) I should go make sure Doug didn't violate this poor man's constitutional rights, (c) the guy is the only black man in a gray shirt running from the direction of the store, (d) hey, stupid, he's the thief, and (e) holy crap, I'm still sitting in the car! Finally, I pulled my head out and ran over to help Doug.

We (and by "we" I mean Doug) got the guy secured as the security guard from the store showed up and positively identified him as the thief. I don't remember a time when I felt so stupid. The guy that I had pictured in my head was much slimmer and younger, and I convinced myself to look for that guy instead of just watching for someone fitting the description given.

A lot of us have missed out on the work Jesus because it isn't what we think it should be. We have an idea in our head, and that is what we keep waiting for. We keep praying for God to use us to change the world, and we expect to be put in glamorous, obvious, to-be-envied-by-all world-saving situations. Maybe we see a need, but "it's not our thing," so we just let it go. We can't be bothered to offer a kind word or act because we are waiting for the *big* one. People who waste their time on small things are less righteous than we are. Our calling is bigger than theirs.

I learned two things from this event. First, don't sit there waiting for something cool to come your way when the guy next to you is fighting for his life. Number two is even simpler: don't criticize another man who is working when all you are doing is watching. It's possible that he is doing the job that you were supposed to do.

LAUGHING MONKEYS

This lady called to report that children were buried in her yard. You don't get many calls like that, and I was beyond excited. I had visions of busting John Wayne Gacy and booking him into jail still dressed in his clown outfit. That's the kind of crap that I just beg to happen every night.

When I arrived, I quickly found out that there were no children. The lady was crazy, and she was seeing children falling out of the trees and disappearing into the grass. Before long, the children in the trees became monkeys.

This poor lady was seeing this, and she legitimately believed what she was seeing. I couldn't be mean to her because, dagnabbit, she didn't choose to be nuts. She was just a sad old lady who had lost her mind. I didn't know what to do but humor her for a few minutes.

The monkeys got out of the tree and got into her car. I walked over to her car and looked in the windows. Then she told me that the monkeys were laughing at me.

How dare those stupid monkeys laugh at me? I was the dang police. No one laughs at me. I was gonna regulate all over some laughing monkeys. Let's see how much those little motorscooters laugh with a size 10 in their anal cavities.

Yeah, I really had those thoughts. I remember being all kinds of riled up. I really got mad at a bunch of imaginary monkeys who were sitting in a car laughing at me.

Fortunately for me, the old lady, and the monkeys, I stopped taking myself so seriously. I got my ego under control and convinced the lady to go inside and go to sleep.

So, about this ego of mine… I don't know what to do with it sometimes.

Not everyone is going to respect us as police officers or as human beings. Some people, and apparently some imaginary monkeys, are missing that part of the brain that gives people the respect that they are due. Our value as people is not dependent upon what some knucklehead says. We can't take ourselves so seriously that we wig out when something bucks our concept of how we should be treated. We also can't take our critics too seriously. Everyone has an opinion. Let us listen to the opinions of the people that actually matter, and let us see the rest as the meaningless laughs of imaginary monkeys locked in a car.

WHAT HAVE YOU DONE FOR ME LATELY?

I met some older cops for breakfast one morning. I was new to their shift, and I thought it would be a good idea to socialize. As we were sitting there, I got a call of a disturbance. I immediately got up and started walking toward the door because breakfast isn't nearly as fun as taking someone to jail. One of the other guys yelled to me as I exited, "That guy likes to carry knives. Be careful." My thought was, *Gee, thanks. If you think I might get stabbed, how about you get up and come help?*

These days, no one has any respect for that cop. He's lazy, irritating, fat, and unreliable. The rumor is that he was the truth back in the day. Fincher, who isn't one to blow smoke, told me that Captain Lazypants was a great cop and someone you always wanted with you as a backup. That tidbit was interesting, but it didn't do me any good when I was dealing with the guy who likes to stab people.

I could tell you all about my Christian exploits of when I was younger and more devout. You might be impressed for a second, but if I still can't produce good work, I'm no good to you. I'm sure God has it written down, and it matters to him what I did fifteen years ago, but he is much more interested in what I am doing for him right dadgum now. He doesn't stand in heaven with a "Recently Impressed Me" sticker to put by my name on his little chart or anything goofy like that. God just wants us to show him that we still love him just as much as we did when we first believed.

JUMP ON IT

A curse on him who is lax in doing the Lord's
work! A curse on him who keeps his sword
from bloodshed!

—Jeremiah 48:10

I realize that if I am not careful, I can take this verse
completely out of context and really jack up the whole
point. To better understand the context from which
this verse comes, you gotta read Jeremiah. I think reading Jeremiah is a drag, to tell you the truth. I'm just not
bright enough to really grasp all of it.

Here is what I get from the verse…

God has called me to fight crime. He has called me
to personally take action and have something to show
for it. Since God has called me to do it, it is the Lord's
work. I better get on it, and I better get my hands dirty.

Whatever God has called you to do, now is the time
to do it.

SKIPPING AND SINGING

During one SWAT training day, the boss got word that there had just been a murder, and the bad guy was on the loose. We were being asked to find him and take him into custody. It was good news for us because all of us really like doing that stuff. It's what we signed up for.

My buddy Dolan's reaction to the news is forever burned in my mind. He began skipping and singing, "We just had a mur-der!" He wasn't happy that someone in our town was killed. He was elated about putting into action all the hours of training and preparing. It was the image of a man loving his calling.

Later that night, Dolan literally made the bad guy crap his pants.

God knows us better than we know ourselves. He has programmed us for his service, and all of the work he has done in our lives will pay off at some point. When we embrace the call that God has for us, we can skip and sing for joy.

We are about to make the devil crap his pants.

I DATED A MARRIED WOMAN

There is a certain camaraderie between cops and convenience store workers. We tend to congregate in their stores for breaks, and they seem to like having us around. Sometimes, you strike up conversations that lead to friendships.

When I was brand-new, I wasn't much of a convenience store congregator. I wasn't much of a break-taker, and I wasn't particularly social. But I had to pee somewhere, and I got hooked on energy drinks. So I would run inside, take a leak, grab a drink, and be out the door.

One clerk was impressed enough with me, for whatever reason, to ask another officer about me. The guy she talked to just happened to be my boss. He knew I was single and a decent person, so he put in a good word with the clerk. Later, he told me to go talk to her. Always one to obey the boss, I did what he said. She asked me on a date, and I agreed, still not even knowing her name. She wasn't wearing a nametag, and I couldn't think of a polite way to ask after she had asked me out. I didn't want to go out, but I didn't have a good excuse handy. Plus, I thought my boss expected me to go with the flow.

STEVEN SANDERS

The evening of the date came. The first clue should have been that she wanted me to pick her up for our date at a Wendy's instead of her house.

Fortunately, I picked up on the second clue. While we were eating supper, she began talking about her kids, and then she mentioned her husband. Now, I wasn't much of a detective, but I heard "my husband" and not "my ex-husband." I stopped her and asked about that, sure that I had just misunderstood.

Oh no, she was married.

Oh, waiter, check, please.

The next time she saw one of my cop buddies, she told him that she thought her having kids had scared me away. No, it was the idea of getting shot over a girl whose name I didn't even know.

My ignorance of her marital status meant that my conscience was clear, and I had not done anything intentionally wrong. I'm sure that my ignorance wouldn't have impressed her husband.

When I stand before God, I don't want to tell him that I just rocked along doing what I thought was right without ever cracking my Bible to see what the truth actually is. We don't have the right to be ignorant about the truth.

DWIGHT

There was a kid I knew in high school named Dwight. Dwight was irritating. I thought he was poorly behaved and was a bit thrown off. He talked about killing things and seemed to try really hard to impress people. For some reason, he liked me and always wanted to talk to me. Not being a total schmuck, I wasn't mean to him, but I also didn't really try to befriend him. I couldn't be bothered to deal with him for long, so I just avoided him whenever possible. I didn't want him to think he should hang out with me, but I also didn't want to hurt his feelings. I was a weird combination of nice and snooty, and I think he just needed someone to give him the time of day.

We did a swat hit on Dwight. He was threatening "suicide by cop," and he had reportedly barricaded himself in his house. He eventually gave up without any trouble, but the whole time the ordeal dragged on, I thought that I should have been nicer to him when we were kids. Maybe God brought him into my life so that I could show him love and avoid this standoff years later. He was just so hard to love.

Loving the unlovable. Jesus asks us to do that, and it's difficult. He knows how difficult it is because he loves us when we are unlovable. He even seeks us out for a relationship with him. No one comes to God without God having drawn that person to himself. We don't have to knock on God's door, he is already knocking on ours.

So yeah, loving annoying people is hard. Try loving every annoying person who has ever or will ever live. We aren't being asked too much.

SOUNDING LIKE JESUS

Geo has been a cop for a few years longer than I have. When I first got out on my own, he was one of the first people to treat me like an equal. I actually owe my disturbance solving theory of "when in doubt, just put someone in jail" to him, but that is beside the point. For a while, every time I said hi to him in my testosterone-heavy voice, he would say, "Dang, Bones Love, you sound like Jesus." My response would always be, "Well, he does live inside of me."

I think my joke is very clever, and it makes me laugh every time. Yes, I laugh at my own jokes. Heck, someone has to laugh at them, right? But why does it have to be a joke? If Jesus does live inside of me, shouldn't I sound like Jesus when I talk?

DISCERNMENT

King Solomon asked God to give him wisdom. I had the belief when I was young, for whatever reason, that Solomon asked God to make him smart. When I grew up and read the Bible passage for myself, I discovered that Solomon didn't ask God to make him the smartest man in the world. He asked for a "discerning heart to govern the people and to distinguish between right and wrong."

Even if you don't have to govern people, being able to distinguish between right and wrong is a trait that we all need to have. Then, if we can just put that knowledge to use...

PARENTING

We smacked a motel room where some nasty people were slinging dope. When we came in, the main dealer acted like he was pulling a gun out of his pants, making Chatwell almost shoot him. It turned out that he was actually trying to hide crack in his pants, but his brain had locked down, and his body just wouldn't cooperate.

Here is the scene: five adults, three kids, one bed, cocaine everywhere, and a steady flow of scumbags in and out of the room. The adults were seated around a table cutting up the dope, and the kids were in bed less than five feet away. As we got them all rounded up, suddenly, one of the criminals asked us to let her check on her kids because she was worried about them… in the bed… with all the cops standing around.

Oh, so now you're worried about your kids? You pick this exact five-minute span of their lives to finally wonder if they are okay? What about the first five years of their lives when you openly used and sold cocaine in front of them and exposed them to the creepiest people in town? Where was your concern then?

I think I said something like, "Your kids are fine now." And then we called CPS. The foster system may suck, but if those kids were going to have any chance of succeeding in life, it would have to be with other adults.

I haven't been a parent very long, so I know that I'm not the expert. I can tell you that selling dope around them is a bad idea.

The first draft of this book had the word "douchebag" in most every chapter. It just seemed like a fitting description for many of the criminals I talked about. I didn't think much of it until I was telling my uncle about the book and its often coarse language. I was mid-sentence when my niece, Ruthie, screamed out, "Douchebag!" She was seven, it was my fault, and it wasn't cute or funny. I did some heavy editing after that.

Jesus talked about how it would be better for someone to die slowly than to lead a small child astray.

I think that sums it up nicely.

A CHOICE TO HELP AND NOT HURT

We had to run over all these mounds of dirt one SWAT practice day. We'd run to the top, shoot some targets, run down, and repeat the process for, like, ever. I was in a group with Chatwell, who I respect and fear. I was running just ahead of him going uphill when I stepped on a rock. My foot slipped, and I kicked Chatwell in the face. I started to fall back, so Chatwell put his hand on my back and steadied me. I got my footing, and we kept running and shooting.

When it was over, I went up to Chatwell, and I very meekly asked him about the boot to the face. He said that his thought process was like this, "Bones just kicked my face. Don't kill Bones. Don't kill Bones. I love Bones. Don't kill Bones." He knew that it was an accident, but it didn't feel good, and his first instinct was to be violent toward the thing that hurt him. As fun as that would have been, we had an objective, and helping me stand up was the way to get everyone to the finish line.

We are all running the same race. People hurt us accidentally and intentionally all the time. We can choose to hurt back, or we can help steady them, get them back on track, and get back in the race. We may not have the ability to help, but we don't have to repay pain for pain.

NOT REALLY MISSED

For some odd reason, I was doing yard work one afternoon on my day off from work. For an even odder reason, I started thinking about a patrol officer who I had not seen at work in a long time. I don't make a habit of doing yard work or thinking about other dudes, but it was apparently a strange day. Anyway, I realized that I hadn't heard him on the radio, seen him around, or even heard a thing about him in forever. When I came back to work, I asked about him. I learned that he had quit a few months prior and moved like 300 miles away. No wonder I hadn't seen him.

Don't be the guy that no one notices is gone. At work, or in life, having no one notice that you have left is a sign that you aren't making much of an impact on the people around you.

EVEN WORSE THAN NOT BEING MISSED

Speaking of not being missed, there was this kid in town that I think all of us had arrested at least once. He was very irritating. He was always stirring up some kind of crap and acting like a knucklehead. One day, he was found dead from an overdose. I was actually happy to hear that he was dead. How Christian is that? Heck, I think everyone at the PD was happy he was dead. If they weren't happy, they at least weren't sad. It's a shame, but that's how it is.

It was a waste of more than twenty years of his life. We only have a set number of days here on Earth, and no one can say for sure just how long we are going to have. It is time to evaluate our lives and see if we have done anything worthwhile. There will be some people who will rejoice when I die, and I can't help that. The question to ask ourselves is, have we done any good with what we have been given? If you don't know, ask someone who knows you. If you can't brainstorm and find a single positive thing you have done, the time to make a change is right dadgum now. You aren't promised any more time to fix things.

SAVING A LIFE PART TWO

I stopped this car, and the driver was drunk. I arrested him and then dealt with his female passenger. I immediately noticed that something was off. She was big, had a very square jaw, and had the manliest hands I had ever seen. I asked her what her name was. She answered, "My name is Frank, but he doesn't know." Oh my.

As a side note, I had a dispatcher riding with me that night. She remembers Frank wearing very short shorts, and she saw why Frank was a Frank long before I did.

The driver had picked up this dude in a bar thinking he was a girl. He was on the way home with him, and he was going to get a very ugly surprise. Fortunately for the driver and his new friend, I stopped and arrested him. I have no doubt that I saved someone's life that night.

Frank looked like a girl at first, but upon closer inspection, it was pretty obvious he was a dude. The lesson here is less of a Biblical one, and more of a lifeical one. Don't get so drunk that you end up sleeping with a dude on accident.

ONE DAY, YOU'RE ON TOP OF THE WORLD

I arrested a guy for driving with a suspended license. It was a righteous charge and arrest, but I could have just as easily written him a ticket. The reasons I arrested him were: (1) I like arresting people, and (2) several other cops and I had just finished fighting another guy, and I was still pretty driven up. My driver seemed pretty sleazy, but he was polite and cooperative. It was a toss-up, so I went with my standard response to the question of "to arrest or not to arrest," and I put him in jail.

My next night off, I was eating supper at Olive Garden. Who should walk by me but the same guy I had put in jail a few days earlier. Of course, he was working there; and of course, I had not yet gotten my food. It was a very vulnerable feeling, knowing that this guy knew me, and he had the chance to pee in my fettuccine.

It's amazing how fast we can go from being the boss to being the bottom feeder. One day, I had all the power, and the next, I was at his mercy. I can't trust in my own power to always save me. One day, I won't be able to be the dang police anymore. I may not even know my own name. What, then, can I trust in to protect me?

The only thing that lasts forever and will never leave us is Jesus. He is also the only real protection that any of us have.

WHAT IS THE POINT?

So you're reading this book and thinking that it doesn't apply to you because you aren't a cop, and you don't even like cops. My illustrations are lost on you, my stories are dumb, my writing is terrible, and you can't imagine who would waste their time with this nonsense. Maybe you just don't get how trying to save a crappy world is important. This verse is for you.

Jeremiah 22:16, "He defended the cause of the poor and needy, and so all went well. Is that not what it means to know me?"

The point is to know and love God. Helping others is the work of God. If you want to do something worthwhile, and you can't seem to get much direction from God, find someone to help and get to work.

SUFFERING

There was this older lady at church who was pretty funny. I had known her for most of my life, but when I became a police officer, she only had one thing to say to me. Whenever she saw me, she would throw her hands up in surrender, laugh and say, "I didn't do it!" Yeah… that joke wasn't funny the first time, and it was even less funny the 837th time.

There was this other girl who came to the PD to try and sell us life insurance or something. I don't know what she was selling because she started off her presentation with a donut joke. After that, I just tuned her out.

When I walk into a room, and someone grabs the person next to them and screams out, "Here he is, take him!," or "He did it!" I do my best to not shoot them both.

I even have some people make jovial pig comments at me, and they think I'm going to laugh with them.

All around the world, other police officers are fighting for their lives. They have to deal with firebombs, real death threats, angry mobs, poor training and equipment, serious corruption, and volatile governments. Here I am, griping about some bad jokes. If that is as bad as it gets for me, I should do a backflip every time I get accused of eating a donut.

For many Christians, some snickering and mockery is all we have to deal with for making our faith known. For others, they have to give up everything—family, money, jobs, their lives—to be a follower of Jesus.

If the worst thing that I have to deal with is being made fun of for believing that some guy was killed on a cross and then came back to life, I'm good.

HELPING A BROTHER OUT

Two of my coworkers just got into a big fight at a bar. One of them started screaming on the radio for help. When I showed up, there were at least twenty cops there. There were state troopers and sheriff's deputies there too. It's not uncommon at all for someone to radio in for help, but yelling into the radio like a banshee that you need more units will get everyone en route. We don't even have to like the guys we are going to help. Heck, I really don't like either of those guys. But when one of us is in trouble, we are all going to go and beat someone down. We might talk badly about one of our coworkers, run them down to our friends, tell them they are a loser, or try to get them fired, but when that same person calls for help, everyone is going to show up ready for war. We take care of our own.

When I was younger, my dad had bladder cancer. The Sunday after we found out, my mom announced to the church that he had cancer, and we were scared. My family has never been the most popular people at church. We're likeable and don't usually stir up drama, but we also like to keep to ourselves and not be too social. I'm sure there were people in the congregation who had run us down behind our backs or thought we were losers. But when my mom asked for help, everyone got up and met us at the front of the church to pray for my dad. Every. Single. Person.

Coming together in a time of need is what the practice of being a Christian is all about. Setting aside personal differences to help each other survive should be the end goal of the church family. We need to take care of our own.

RIGHT AND WRONG

I caught a guy breaking into a church. He had stolen a bunch of Bibles and was sitting at the pastor's desk. My first thought was to let him go. Shoot, the dude obviously needed a Bible. He really needed to read it too. My mind was going really fast, and I thought about if I didn't arrest him, maybe he would come back to that church and get saved. Maybe he was the next Billy Graham, and all he needed was some mercy.

It was a very fast debate, and I had to make a decision. Arrest the guy and send him to hell, or cut him loose and possibly save his soul. I'm getting paid to enforce the law, but maybe the church would turn the other cheek. There was no one else to ask, so it was all on me to decide.

Dude went to jail.

It may not have been very Christian-like, but there is right and wrong in the world. If he needed a Bible, he could come back during business hours and be given one. The guy begged me to let him go, and his reason was that he had been out of prison for only one day. What had he gone down for? Burglary, of course. Yeah, dude, that fool needed to go back. I wasn't a jerk about it. In fact, I was really nice to him. I just explained that he had done wrong, and that was it.

Someone has to be the voice of right and wrong. Christians don't have to be doormats and let people with evil intentions just run over them. I know we are supposed to turn the other cheek, and I don't understand how everything fits together, but I'm not gonna let anyone break into my house and steal.

We have an obligation to take a stand for what is right. People who want to do wrong may tell us that we are imposing on them, but that doesn't change things. If we have an actual responsibility over a situation, we have to be the ones to make sure the right thing is done.

If the people supposedly inhabited by the spirit of God can't find the testicular fortitude to stand up to evil, we're all screwed.

SUICIDE

The best suicide I ever worked happened on an otherwise quiet morning. You know the person telling the story is a bit throwed off when he begins the story with "The best suicide I ever worked." I am what I am. Anyway, this old guy had been sick for a long time. He called his ex-wife and asked her to come over and help him for a little while. When she showed up, the front door was unlocked, so she walked inside.

Her ex-husband was sitting in a chair only a few feet away, facing her. Well, he wasn't really facing her, per se, because he didn't have much of a face. Everything above his nostrils was gone. Well, it wasn't gone. It was all over the floor, walls, and ceiling.

He had called her, gotten himself set up, put a powerful gun in his mouth, pulled the trigger, and made sure that his parting gesture to his ex-wife was more potent than any middle finger could ever be. I wonder if she ever sleeps.

First off, if any of you guys find inspiration in this and copy what that wanker did, I will find you in the afterlife and kick you.

Second, killing yourself is a real tacky thing to do. It screws with people for a long time. There is no making up afterward. You're dead, and everyone else has to live with wondering if they were the catalyst who killed you.

I don't know how killing yourself affects your eternal salvation, but I do know how it affects what you leave behind—it screws it all up.

If you are considering suicide, do you really want the thing people remember you for is that you killed yourself? That's a pretty lame epitaph.

I GOT RUNNED OVER

I rolled up on a disturbance when I was still in training. The victim was a moderately sized dude who at first looked like he wanted to fight me. He jumped out of his truck, came around the hood, and started walking aggressively toward me. I got out of my police car ready to box, and he suddenly fell to his knees and began screaming, "I got runned over!" I was a wee bit confused.

Apparently, he and his wife had been arguing. She had been sitting in her car, trying to leave. He was standing at her window, probably acting like a dufus. She put the car in gear, and because he was leaning on the vehicle, he fell over. According to him, one tire ran over his forearm as his wife sped away into the sunset. As a result, he was weeping and wailing like a little girl, literally, about having been "runned over."

There was not a mark on him, by the way. He had apparently been okay enough to get into a pickup and wait for me to show up, but what do I know? He was transported to the ER because he kept screaming about how much agony he was in. Go figure; the medical exam showed absolutely no damage. The prevailing thought among all of us was that he was either full of crap or the biggest weenie on Earth.

I had the privilege of uncovering the truth a few months later. I arrested the same guy for some warrants. At the time, his other arm was in some kind of bandage. After all the whining and crying about how the handcuffs were going to hurt him, it was clear that he was just a big fat wuss.

Some people just aren't tough, and that's fine with me. I'm not really all that tough. I wouldn't care about how big of a pansy he was except that I had also seen him in another setting, and he acted much differently. I had gone to a pro wrestling event (note: it isn't called a "show" to true believers like me—it's a dadgum event), and he was there. He was wearing a Stone Cold Steve Austin shirt. Had Stone Cold known who was wearing his shirt, he would have given himself a Stone Cold Stunner out of pure shame. This guy was bowing up to the wrestlers, challenging them to fight him. If I was more mature, I would have rolled me eyes and let it go. Instead, I began yelling to the rest of the crowd about how big of a pantywaist he actually was. I don't think he heard me, but the people in front of me did, and they found it very amusing. At least I could educate someone.

We can portray ourselves however we want to, but the truth is still the truth. God knows who we are when we are by ourselves. It is that person, the one that only God knows, that is actually who we are.

ZOMBIES

This one isn't about police work. It was a thought that I stole from my wife. But since I have spent hours of my career telling cohabitating couples that Texas says whatever they own is community property, her idea is now my idea.

My wife loves zombie movies. They freak her out, but she watches them whenever she can't find any reruns of *Dance Moms*, *Property Brothers*, or *Love It Or List It*. Because I'm a loving and supportive husband, I watch the zombie movies with her. I'm not a fan, mostly because I don't like being scared, and I don't usually like movies without lots of kung fu and subtitles.

The other day, my wife turned to me and said that lots of people are zombies. Zombies aren't necessarily mean. They aren't even bad. Zombies are just selfish. All they do is feed themselves. They only care about getting their next meal, and they are never satisfied.

How do people deal with zombies? They either run away or shoot them in the head. No one likes zombies. Even zombie fans really wouldn't want to hang out with one in real life. They aren't good for conversation because all they think about is themselves; you can't play with them because they will eat you, and you can't put them to work because they will constantly wander off in search of brains. Zombies aren't good for anything.

Don't be a zombie. No one will like you.

POOR CLARK

Moeller pulled over a car that was being driven by this kid I knew from church. The kid named Clark was wearing what appeared to be a wedding ring, and Moeller thought that it was odd for a 16-year-old kid to be married. It turned out that the ring was part of the *True Love Waits* program that Clark had attended at church. Then Clark mentioned me. Moeller called me to see if Clark was fibbing, so I decided to swing by the stop.

When I arrived, Moeller had just kicked Clark loose. I had a sudden, and totally uncontrollable, evil thought. I flashed my flashlight at Clark's side mirror, and he stopped. I sprinted up to the car, making sure that I stomped my feet as hard as I could. When I reached the rear bumper, I screamed, "Get your hands up!" in my manliest and scariest voice. By the time I was even with his window, Clark had his hands on the roof, his mouth was gaping open, his eyes were like saucers, and a tiny and terrified cry escaped his shaking body.

In a moment, I was both rolling on the ground, laughing, and feeling a bit sad. It was a weird combination. My prank was very funny, and the look on Clark's face was unbelievably awesome, but it still made me a little sad to scare the poor guy like that.

He was a good sport. He, still shaken, told me that I had "scared the (slang term for poop)" out of him. I laughed an evil laugh as I walked back to Moeller, who was also laughing. Clark drove away and probably had nightmares about a bald-headed guy in polyester screaming at him.

It was probably an abuse of power, but it was a lot of fun.

Many of us pick on the people we like. I don't know why we do that, but one way that we show acceptance and appreciation is to make fun of each other. I wonder if God does that to us. I think some people have the idea that God is boring, and heaven will be the dullest place ever. I don't know if God will prank us for eternity, but I do know that heaven will be a blast. I am sure of that because God is the author of our happiness, and I bet he loves to make us laugh.

NOBODY'S GOT IT ALL TOGETHER

Nickell and I were at the range one night on a secret mission to recover something that I had accidentally left there the previous week. It's good for airheads to have friends with keys to the range. Unfortunately, Nickell didn't have the one key to the one room where the one thing I really needed was being kept. But he knew someone who did. He left me at the range with the promise that he would return soon with the key.

The range is dark, and it's secluded; and I watch way too many zombie movies, thanks to my wife. I was walking around in the dark parking lot playing with my fancy phone to distract myself. It wasn't working, and I was soon sure that I was seeing zombies coming at me from the shadows.

When Nickell showed back up, he found me standing in the bed of my pickup, on top of the toolbox. He got out of his car and said, "Bones, you ar-ite?" I told him that I was. It wasn't a lie because I was very much ar-ite now that I wasn't left alone to be eaten by zombies. He knew I was full of crap, so he asked me if I was standing up there to get better phone reception.

I started to agree with his explanation because the truth was exceptionally lame. But it was Nickell. There are only a few people at work to whom I can bare my soul, and he is one of them. So my answer was, "I was standing there because I was scared of being attacked by zombies. I figured that if I was on my toolbox, I could see them and shoot them before they could sneak up on me."

Nickell just laughed and shook his head. It's just the kind of off-the-wall crap he has come to expect from me over the years.

As Christians, we can't expect people to believe anything we say if we lie about small things. In Jill Phillips's song called *Nobody's Got It All Together*, I get that we should be honest about our shortcomings because we are all in the same boat of imperfection. So yeah, sometimes I have a totally irrational fear of being eaten by a herd of zombies. That is probably the least weird thing about me. I want people to know Jesus through the way I live my life, and that can't happen if I pretend to be the perfect little Christian with all of the world's problems figured out. I think overall that people respond better to honesty, no matter how goofy it is, than to a show.

The glory of God is made perfect in our weakness, even if our weakness is lame.

LEADERSHIP

There are lots of supervisors at the PD. The best ones, I think, are the ones who work alongside their troops. They know how their guys work because they are right there with them. I can't think of a better way to influence or supervise others than to actually work with them.

When I worked for Hedrick, he was always in the fight with us. Hedrick pushed us to work harder, not by griping at us from behind a desk, but by doing what he expected us to do. He answered calls, took reports, made arrests, and worked wrecks. If someone needed a beating, he was there with us to dish one out. He, Doug, Sharp, and I wrestled this guy on a bed late one night. There were probably too many of us fighting in one tiny room, but none of us were going to let someone else do our fighting for us. Sharp spider-monkeyed his head, Doug and Hedrick grabbed for his arms, and I latched onto his legs. My head ended up on the dude's butt, and it was only covered by his tighty whities. During the scuffle, Hedrick reached back and accidentally elbowed Doug in the head, nearly knocking him out. Good times!

We had no choice but to respect Hedrick. It was always a battle for me and Doug to beat him to calls. He let us work and make our own decisions and often just acted like a back-up officer. I can testify from experience that Hedrick's mere presence made bad guys act differently, and that made things easier for us.

Hedrick didn't expect or ask us to do anything that he himself wouldn't do. That made all the difference in our work ethic. We would have done anything for him.

Jesus isn't sitting in heaven, just watching us and playing chess with little clay versions of us. He doesn't take naps, get distracted, or become too busy for us. He is actively at work with us right now. We don't have to wait for him to show up and save the day because he is already there. Pretty often, he is doing all of the work and letting us think that we are the ones making things happen. I think that at other times, he is standing by, proudly watching as his children handle business and use what he has taught them to overcome adversity. Jesus doesn't ask us to do anything that he wouldn't do himself. He's already done it all anyway.

It's easy to follow a leader like that.

TWO

'm one of the guys on our SWAT team who is trained to shoot gas into a house. We had to go through a week-long school where we were gassed every day with some chemical agent. The word is that we have to be exposed so that we know what it does. I think it's more of a rite of passage.

My first time in the barrel was on call where a guy barricaded himself in a fairly nice house owned by his parents. We gave him chances to come out, but he just wouldn't. As things progressed, the boss decided to gas the wanker. I was the guy holding the gas gun.

Oh yes.

During that fancy school, we learned a mathematical formula so that we wouldn't accidentally kill someone by using too much gas. I don't do math worth a hoot, and the teacher realized that most of us weren't in police work because long division got us excited, so he gave us two very important tips. First, OC (pepper gas) doesn't have an actual lethal dosage. Second, if you are in doubt, just shoot two rounds of gas in every window. Sweet! I can count to two.

To this day, I still get mocked for my performance that day. Garza and Dolan were covering me while I pumped gas into the house. I had counted out exactly the number of rounds I was going to need based on the number of windows, including a tiny bathroom window. They kept telling me, "Bones, that's a small window and a small room. Are you sure you want two rounds in it?" and I just kept repeating, "Two in every window." *Bang... Bang.* Next window, please. Like I said, I can count to two.

Mock my very literal translation of the rules all you want, but that wanker came running out of the house in surrender soon after.

When Jesus was asked what the greatest commandment was, he gave an answer that the people asking did not expect. He said, "Love the Lord your God with all your heart, mind, soul, and strength. This is the first and greatest commandment. The second is like it. Love your neighbor as yourself." In doing that, Jesus summed up all of the Bible into two steps. Because of that, we don't have to memorize seven million pages of rules and rituals in order to do the work of God. We have to: (1) Love God, and (2) Love everyone else.

When the question arises about how God wants us to live and act, all we have to do is count to two.

POLYESTER

There is a civilian employee at the PD who is made fun of all the time behind her back. Sometimes I think we are all stuck in junior high.

This one schmuck cop was hating on her to his buddies. He told a story about how he had been talking to her when he slipped and called her by her less-than-gratifying secret nickname that he had made up for her. They all had a good laugh at her expense.

She likes to wear polyester. That's the whole joke. Seriously. The joke is polyester.

Hey, butthole, that fancy police uniform that you wore for twenty years? It's freaking polyester, you idiot. You disgrace it with your needless mockery of someone who was forced to put up with you much longer than anyone should have to. You didn't deserve to wear polyester. The fact that you and I have worn identical uniforms at any point makes me embarrassed.

Do any of us really have the right to make fun of other people? I do it often, and I am usually reminded that I'm a jerk for doing it. God has made me go up to people that I was mean to over the years, confess my meanness, and ask for their forgiveness. It sucks, and you'd think I'd just stop running people down by now.

Nope, I'm usually the wanker assigning secret nicknames and poking fun at people who are more worthy of grace than I will ever be. Maybe that butthole and I deserve to wear identical uniforms after all. Please excuse me while I punch myself in the face.

ROY

Some moron who called himself "El Diablo" posted a bunch of stuff on the Internet about how he was going to kill all of Midland PD and their families. He even threatened the chief of police's daughter by name. That's a real good way to end up with a bunch of angry and well-armed people at your doorstep. Go figure; that's what happened, and he's in jail.

Roy, an oilfield worker who has only known me for a few years, read about El Diablo. He gave me a call the other night just to say that he was praying for me and my family. He's an exceptionally nice guy who loves Jesus and prays very honest prayers. Then Roy told me about this new rifle that he had bought and how I was welcome to come out to his house, set up a stronghold, and shoot anyone who wanted to harm me.

I can't think of any words to describe how awesome that was to hear. Every time I think about that, I just nod my head because words can't do it justice.

God loves his children, and he is going to take care of us. I'm sure he gets really irritated when people want to hurt us. God will take care of us, and bad guys will pay. There is someone who sees the right and wrong, and someday he will make all things right.

HI, MY NAME IS BONES

Many of us at the PD have nicknames that have stuck for years. Mort, General, Whiskey, Shane, Fern, Head, Snatch, Riki Bobbi, Frog, Spanky, Hoss, Rusty, Big Worm, Mac, and T-Weezy are the first ones that come to mind. My nickname is Bones. I used to be very skinny, and an old sergeant decided to name me for my thinness. It just happened one night in briefing. Nickell was the first to catch on and spread it. Soon, everyone from the big chief down to the newest rookies were calling me Bones. Before long, CPS workers, Midland County guys, guys in the next county, and federal agents only knew me as Bones. Most of them don't know my real name, actually. Fortunately, it isn't a bad name. The only problem now is that people have to ask me why I have that name. I'm not quite as bone-ish as I once was.

Assigning someone a nickname is often a sign of acceptance. It can also be the opposite of acceptance, but it's pretty obvious. Names I give people can be subtle and lame, like Douglas, Mikey, or Kenny Wayne, or it can be awesome like Whiplash or Timtimmerie Timtimmerie Tim Tim Terie. Yes, I really call someone that. I haven't given Hedrick, Chatwell, Fincher, or Herman nicknames. They might hate them and kill me. As a side note, I'm so terrified of Lt. Land that she is the only person that I always call by her official title.

Revelation 2:17 says, "To him who overcomes, I will give some of the hidden manna. I will also give him a white stone with a new name written on it, known only to him who receives it." That's Jesus talking. He has a name assigned to us that only he and us, individually, will know, and he wants to give it to us. Don't you see? Jesus knows you personally, and he has personally named you with a name that fits only you. My thinking is that it has to be a name that echoes the essence of the relationship we have with Jesus. I hope my name is awesome, and I hope I live up to it today.

ASK AND BE READY FOR THE ANSWER

Last week, another officer called me with a question. The officer wanted to know what to do with a certain situation they were facing. The solution, I was told, was one of two things. I gave my answer, which was one of the two options I was given. The officer's response was, "I'm not going to do that."

I'm not always right, and I didn't take it personally that my advice was not accepted. I was, however, annoyed that I was asked advice with a multiple choice answer, but one of the choices wasn't really a choice. I'm just a dude, and personal discretion is a big part of this job; but the point is, if there are two choices and you ask me which direction to go, it's a 50/50 chance that I will pick the answer you like less. If you are not willing to do one of the two things on the table, then you shouldn't be asking anyone what to do.

I can't count how many times I have prayed for God's will to be done. Several of those times, what I meant was actually, "God, do what I want you to do."

The goofiest part is, I've actually gotten mad at God for not picking the answer I wanted him to pick.

If we are not willing to bend our will to the will of God, don't waste his time asking for his help. Asking God to bless our current endeavor and asking God to direct us are two separate things. That being said, asking for God's blessing is never a bad thing. We should just be ready when he doesn't get on board with our stupid idea, and he tells us to change.

SUNSETS

I worked out with the police academy class a few years ago, and I was talking with a few of them afterward. One of the recruits said to me, "Hey, do you remember me? You arrested me a while back."

Of all the things I expected to hear at the *police* academy, "You arrested me" never crossed my mind. He went on to explain that I arrested him for some dinky warrants, and he told me on the way to jail that he had been thinking about becoming a cop. He figured his dreams were over, but I told him to give it a shot anyway. I was nice to him, and he told me that I pretty much talked him into testing for the PD after he got out of jail.

Turns out, that kid is a heckuva cop. He works dang hard, does good work, has a really good attitude, and he likes pro wrestling. It took being arrested to get him back on track, and it's a good thing for the PD.

When the sun sets here in Midland, the sky and clouds turn gold, pink, and purple. The word I heard is that all the color changes are caused by pollution. I have no idea if that is correct, but it doesn't have to be for me to make an illustration. The sunset is made beautiful when the sun shines through bad stuff in the air.

Sin pollutes our lives, but God can use it for our good. He can also turn our mistakes into proof of his goodness. Don't let your ugliness keep you from God. He wants to use your past to make you beautiful.

When the Son shines through our imperfections, it's a work of art.

VIOLENCE IS NEVER THE ANSWER

Recently at a work meeting, I was eavesdropping on a conversation between two non-police women. Apparently, one of them was having trouble with her kid wanting to fight people. She explained that she told her kid, "Violence is never the answer." I couldn't help myself, so I piped in with, "Yes it is." Unimpressed, she looked at me and repeated herself. I wasn't going to win that argument.

Sorry, lady. Violence is often the answer.

Some people only respond to violence. It's all they know. Years ago, I fought this bad guy and dropped him on his face, leaving him with a minor injury. He wanted to complain to my boss about me being too violent with him. Hedrick showed up, and the bad guy's demeanor changed immediately. Unbeknownst to me, this same bad guy had fought Hedrick once before, and it had not gone well for the bad guy. Seeing who my boss was, he no longer wanted to complain; he just wanted to go to jail. I've dealt with the guy since then, and he hasn't fought me anymore.

I don't know how all of this talk of violence fits with Jesus telling us to turn the other cheek. I do know that God has called his people to fight many times in history. When Jesus comes back to Earth, it's going to be very violent. His violence is going to bring all the evil in the world to its knees.

Should I sit by and be peaceful when someone goes into a school and starts shooting little kids? Should I quote John Lennon when terrorists invade this country? Should I turn the other cheek to a guy coming into my house to hurt me and my family?

There has to be a time for Christians to be violent. I'm not talking about blowing up buildings or tormenting murderers, but the world is falling apart, and we have to be willing to fight or die. When violence is the only language your enemy speaks, you might have to speak it back to him.

HERE'S THE STORY

I went to college with a plan to get buff and then become a professional wrestler. I didn't get buff. I also started really wanting to change the world. I figured that play fighting in tights would be awesome, but I would probably not make much impact on society. John Cena, Mick Foley, and a bunch of others have done great things for kids by using their celebrity status as pro wrestlers. I don't have one ounce of their charisma. Since I had also always wanted to be the dang police, I focused on that.

During my last semester of college, I applied for Midland PD. I was sure they were going to hire me. I had learned all about police work in school, and I had all the right answers as to how to change the world. I also had very long hair. Those qualities helped me not get hired.

I switched gears and focused on something else. I had done a lot of preaching in college, and I thought I'd make a great missionary. This missionary company came to my church and begged for people to sign up. He said, "We will take anyone." I applied. He meant, "We will take anyone *except* Steven Sanders." In fact, the organization sent me a rejection e-mail that should have been titled "The Top 10 Reasons Why We Hate You."

How could all of these people be missing the boat on the greatest thing since sliced cheese? I had all the answers, and I was the best candidate for Savior of the World.

I got a job at a bank. My favorite bank story is the day that I let the bank run out of money. Yep. That was my contribution to the financial world. My other favorite story is when I accidentally caused a tidal wave of very cold water to douse the bank president's secretary. The only actual benefits from working there were the friends I made, specifically Jose and Angie, and I learned a little humility. Okay, I learned a lot about humility, actually.

I applied for the PD again, armed with a new outlook and a buzzed hairdo. I got hired. Finally, a break.

The first day of field training, I knew exactly why I was born.

There is no telling how I would have turned out if I had been hired the first time. I had to learn that I didn't know anything before I could actually be taught something.

God's plan isn't always our plan. The end result may be the same, but the road getting there may be different from what we had in mind. If God has shown you your calling, trust him to get you there. It may not be what you thought it would be, but it will be much better.

RELIABILITY

We did a SWAT hit yesterday on this dirtbag. He was reportedly armed with a whole bunch of guns and was very jumpy. According to the intel, he slept in the daytime. This all came from Mitch, who has been working dope and SWAT for like twenty years. I usually prefer to swat people (yes, I just used a noun as a verb) at night when we have the cover of darkness during our approach to the house. Mitch was sure that the guy would be asleep in the daytime, and we needed to hit him before the sun went down.

Who were we hitting? Count Dracula? I was just hoping it wasn't one of those dorky vampires from *Twilight*. I'd hate to wade through the hordes of teenage girls to put boots to the wanker.

We trusted Mitch and hit the house. Just as promised, he was in bed. It worked well for us because the wanker had an assault rifle ready to go in the living room.

I had been a little uneasy about the hit before we got there. I was ready to go and very excited to be there, but I wasn't sure I believed that we were doing it at the best time. As it turns out, Mitch knew what he was talking about.

God is even more reliable than Mitch. He has an immeasurable amount of experience. He is always right. He exists outside of time, so he sees everything and knows how it will all work out. God is trustworthy. He won't lead you astray, and he will always do what is right. God defines reliability.

JUSTIFICATION

Woe to those who call evil good and good
evil, who put darkness for light and light for
darkness, who put bitter for sweet and sweet
for bitter.

—Isaiah 5:20

I was called out to do the fancy detective thing on a
burglary where this dude forced his way into an apartment to try to romance the girl inside. The kicker was
that he was her brother.

Gross.

I jumped into the patrol car with him and told him
that I understood. My reasoning was that every brother
has strange feelings for his sister, and it's easy to confuse
sexual feelings with brother-sister feelings. He took the
bait and confessed. I got out of the car asking myself
what was wrong with me that I would even think to say
something like that.

For the record, I do not feel romantically toward
either of my sisters, and I think people who are hot for
their siblings need lots of help.

One trick in getting a confession is to make what is evil sound not so evil. Once you blur the line between good and evil, there is no reason not to confess. We justify the bad guy's actions to him so that he will give us enough rope to hang him.

We can justify our actions to ourselves pretty easily. I do bad crap, but I know why I do it, so it isn't so bad after all. The devil wants us to do that. He wants us to justify our terrible actions so that he can ruin us. Once we confuse good and evil, there is no reason not to do evil. And that is what is killing mankind.

A GREAT ENDING NOTE

My buddy killed a guy. It was in the line of duty and out of self-defense. I'm proud of my friend for winning a fight for his life. When I heard the news about the dead guy, my response was a very Christian, "——that mother——. I hope he burns in hell."

True story.

I take attacks on cops very personally. Still, "I hope he burns in hell." Really? The guy needed to die that night, no question about it. So yeah, screw him. The problem with me wanting him to go to hell is that Jesus created that wanker, and then he died so that same wanker could go to heaven. It has to hurt Jesus to send people to hell, which is an eternity of suffering and complete separation from God. To wish that on someone, even someone who seemingly deserves it, is to wish pain on Jesus.

Just a few hours later in church, I sobbed like a little girl. I realized the scope of what I had hoped and just how much I meant it. When had I gotten so callous that I wanted Jesus to suffer?

God, help me love you more.